The World of Motorcycles

AN ILLUSTRATED ENCYCLOPEDIA

COLUMBIA HOUSE/New York

Editor: Ian Ward
Editorial Director: Brian Innes
Assistant Editors: Laurie Caddell
Brian Laban
John Tipler
Editorial Assistants:
Caroline Williams
David Vivian
Art Editor: David Goodman
Picture Editor: Mirco Decet
Special Consultants:
Wade Hoyt
Sylvia Netherland
Design: Harry W. Fass
Production: Stephen Charkow
Cover Photos: Phil Mather
A. Morland
J. Greening

contributors
CYRIL AYTON: Commercial bikes
ALAN BAKER: Chain
Clutch
Cornering
STEWART BOROUGHS: Collins
ROY BUCHANAN: CCM
Cheney
ANDREW EDWARDS: Crump
GRAEME EWENS: Croxford
FRANK GLENDINNING: Cleveland
Cotton
STEVE HARVEY: Cecotto
Clothes
DOUG JACKSON: Casal
Cimatti
Cossack
BRIAN LABAN:
Contact breaker adjustment

VITTORIO MARELLI:
Carburettor adjustment
Controls
PHIL MATHER: Customising
BRUCE PRESTON:
Cycle & Motor Cycle Traders' Union
L.J.K. SETRIGHT: Carburettor
Combustion
Compression ratio
Connecting rod
Crankshaft
ERIC THOMPSON: Chater Lea
FRANS VANDENBROEK: Castro
DAVID BURGESS WISE: Clyno
Coventry
Eagle

Picture acknowledgments
Page 241: D. Morley—242: T. Matthews/
Orbis—244: M. M. Rathore—246: M. Decet;
L. J. Caddell—247: M. M. Rathore—248:
Orbis—249: Orbis—250: D. Jackson—251:
P. Dobson; D. Jackson—252: P. Dobson—
253: P. Dobson—254: DPPI—255: J. Greening—
255: J. Greening—256: J. Greening—257:
N. Nicholls; P. Dobson—258: J. Starr;
P. Dobson—259: Orbis—260: P. Dobson—
261: E. Beintema 262/263: DPPI—264:
A. Morland—265: Renolds; Orbis—266:
T. Meeks; L. J. Caddell/Orbis; L. J.
Caddell/Orbis—267: Renolds—268: Motor
Cycle—269: N. Nicholls; National Motor
Museum—270: P. Dobson—271: P. Smith/
Orbis—272/273: J. Greening—274/275:
J. Greening—276: B. Watson/Orbis—277:
D. Jackson—278: D. Burgess Wise—279:
National Motor Museum—280: National
Motor Museum—281: L. J. Caddell/Orbis—
282: Elly Beintema—283: L. J. Caddell/
Orbis—284: Motor Cycle Competition—285:
M. Rathore—286: T. Matthews/Orbis—287:
M. Rathore—288: B. Mayor—289:
T. Matthews/Orbis—290: T. Matthews/Orbis;

BMW—291: L. J. Caddell/Orbis—292:
J. Leech/Orbis; D. Burgess Wise—293:
L. J. Caddell/Orbis—294: National Motor
Museum—295: D. Morley—296/297:
T. Meeks—298: Quattroruote—299: Orbis/
J. Spencer Smith—300/301: T. Rogers/
Orbis/Quattroruote—302: Quattroruote—
303: National Motor Museum/RAC—304:
Keystone—305: National Motor Museum—
306: National Motor Museum; GPO;
Olyslager Organisation—307/308: Orbis—
309: L. J. Caddell/Orbis; Orbis—310:
P. Dobson—311: L. J. Caddell/Orbis—
312: M. Rathore—313: Orbis—314:
M. Rathore; M. Rathore; BMW—315:
Orbis—316/317: Orbis—318: L.J. K.
Setright—319: L. J. Caddell/Orbis; L. J.
Caddell—320: Honda—321: L. J. Caddell/
Orbis—323: Orbis—324: BMW—325: D.
Jackson—326: J. Leech/Orbis—327:
J. Leech/Orbis—328: D. Jackson—329:
D. Jackson—330: L. J. Caddell/Orbis—331:
L. J. Caddell/Orbis—332: P. Dobson—333:
N. Nicholls; Blandford Press—334: Cotton;
Gloucester Citizen; National Motor Museum
—335: J. Greening; R. Maby/Orbis; Cotton
—336: N. Nicholls—337: Cotton—338/339:
B. Watson—340: National Motor
Museum—341: M. Rathore—342/343: B.
Mayor—344: M. Rathore; B. Mayor—345:
B. Holder—346: B. Holder; D. Morley—347:
T. Meeks; D. Morley—348: T. Meeks—349:
Phil Mather—350: Phil Mather—352/353:
Phil Mather—354: Phil Mather; A. Morland—
355: J. Greening—356/357: Phil Mather—
358: B. Preston—359: Motor Cycle; L. J.
Caddell/Orbis—360: L. J. Caddell/Orbis

We are grateful to Mobyke Accessories
Ltd., Rivetts of Leytonstone, Britax,
Kangol and Centurion for the loan of the
clothing which appears in this volume.
We are also grateful to the Myreton Museum,
Aberlady, Scotland, for allowing us to
photograph the Clyno which appears on pages
291 and 293 and to Keith Manning for the
clutch photographs.

Contents   Page

THE MACHINES
Casal	250
CCM	256
Chater Lea	268
Cimatti	276
Cleveland	278
Clyno	291
Commercial bikes	304
Cossack	325
Cotton	332
Coventry Eagle	337

THE BLUEPRINT
Carburettor	241
Chains	264
Clutch	285
Combustion	297
Compression ratio	307
Connecting rod	309
Cooling	318
Crankshaft	341

THE MEN
Castro	254
Cecotto	261
Cheney	272
Collins	295
Croxford	345
Crump	347
Cycle & Motor Cycle Traders Union	358

THE WORKSHOP
Carburettor adjustment	247
Contact breaker maintenance	312
Controls	315
Customising	349

THE LAW
Clothing	281
Cornering	321

GLOSSARY
CONVERSION CHARTS

Feeding the Engine

Paint by
Auto Art
waltham X. 38032.

Norton

The purpose of a carburettor is to provide means whereby the engine can draw the mixture of fuel and air that it requires for combustion, and whereby the rider can control that supply so as to control the performance of the engine. Until a very few years ago, cost consciousness kept motor cycle carburettors remarkably simple in view of the complexity of their task: only very recently have they begun, under the influence of emission legislation rather than of customer demand, to imitate the complication that has become endemic in car carburettors. The earlier and simpler instruments were remarkably efficient when they were new, although the conditions in which they worked often caused them to wear rapidly and lose much of that efficiency. Moreover, the priority traditionally attached by the motor cyclist to his motor has ensured the endurance of a fashion for a separate carburettor for each cylinder, in the cause of good breathing and volumetric efficiency; and now that the modern motor cycle carburettor is often a complex instrument, its multiple application to modern multi-cylinder engines accounts for considerable bulk, weight, and expense – so considerable that a fuel injection apparatus might show advantages. Nevertheless, fuel injection has been almost universally eschewed, the only noteworthy exceptions being a prototype roadgoing version of the four-cylinder Yamaha 750 two-stroke in the 1970s and some racing BMW flat-twin four-strokes dating from the mid 1950s. Whether by injection or by carburation, the object should be the same; but the simple statement of purpose set out above in the very first sentence points out the essential difference between the two systems: injection apparatus is designed to give the engine what it should have, the carburettor allows it to take what it needs. Whether the carburettor succeeds in supplying those wants will depend on its design, its adjustment, and the treatment it is given.

Consider the base chemical nature of the mixture it must supply. It is possible to define a stoichiometric or chemically correct mixture as one which will burn completely inside the engine, producing an exhaust composed almost entirely of nitrogen and carbon dioxide. This mixture contains one part of petrol to some fifteen parts of air by weight. It will not do for all circumstances, however. If economy be desired, the mixture may be weakened (that is, the proportion of petrol reduced) by about 12% at a cost in power of about 7%. Enrich it by 25% and the power will be increased by 4% or thereabouts, the exact figures depending on the aromatic properties of the petrol (which will vary according to the manufacturer and, in most brands, according to the season of the year) and the detonative propensities of the engine. These variations of mixture strength represent the feasible limits for all but the most extraordinary experimental engines; any further weakening or richment can only do harm.

It is clear from this that the carburettor must be capable of supplying an appropriately adjusted and accurate mixture according to the rider's demand for more power or frugality. Its task is made more difficult by the complexities of providing for good combustion, variable engine speed and correspondingly variable volumetric efficiency, changes in atmospheric density and temperature, variations in engine temperature, disturbances to the motor cycle's equilibrium caused by braking or acceleration and the need for reliable starting and idling. All these factors affect the engine's fuel requirements in addition to those which remain constant in any given example – such as air filters, silencers or emission-control devices.

None of these things presents any insuperable difficulties, but until fairly recently there was no single carburettor that coped satisfactorily with them all. The carburettor was still viewed as it had been at the dawn of motor cycling: an essentially simple device that worked well enough for the cost of improving it to be more than most customers would pay. Only when legislation was introduced to control exhaust emissions did the carburettor begin to blossom in all the complexity and comprehensive competence that had so long been latent in it, and even then this display of sophistication was for a long time limited to car carburettors, and is still the exception rather than the rule in motor cycles.

In the earliest forms of the instrument such refinement would have been impossible because of the crudity of early engines. There were in those days carburettors working on principles that have long been abandoned: the surface carburettor, relying on evaporation of petrol from a wick or from a number of soaked wooden balls, was one such, capable of working with the very light petrols available at the turn of the century but not now. The basis of the modern carburettor was, nevertheless, to be found in the earliest petrol-engined vehicles, over ninety years ago: the prototype Daimler bicycle and the Butler tricycle. This was the 'spray' carburettor, working on the scent-spray principle, with or without the refinement of a needle jet such as became commonplace on motor cycles by the turn of the century.

Like all modern instruments, the primitive carburettor made use of a venturi or choke – a constriction, more or less

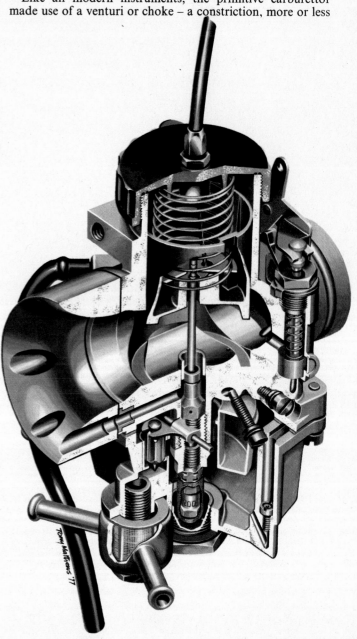

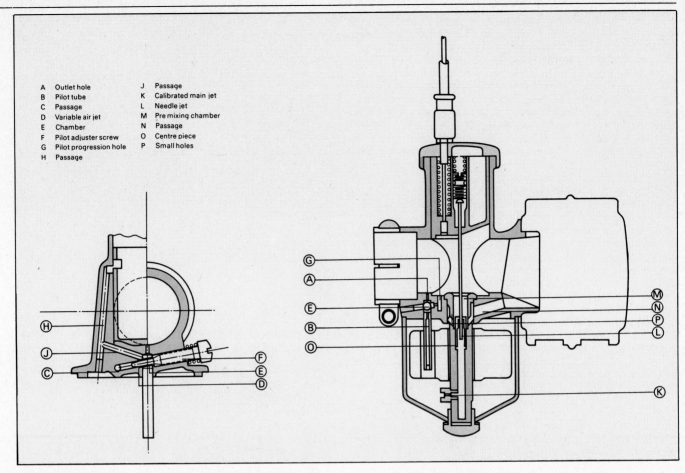

A Outlet hole
B Pilot tube
C Passage
D Variable air jet
E Chamber
F Pilot adjuster screw
G Pilot progression hole
H Passage
J Passage
K Calibrated main jet
L Needle jet
M Pre mixing chamber
N Passage
O Centre piece
P Small holes

streamlined in shape, in the pipe whereby air is admitted to the engine's inlet port or ports. This venturi displays a phenomenon noted in the study of elementary thermodynamics: when a gas blows through a duct, its velocity is highest and pressure lowest at the point of minimum cross-sectional area. It is the engine's business to induce the flow of air; what the venturi does is to create an artificially strengthened suction which can draw a flow of petrol into the air stream at the point of minimum pressure. It would not do to pour the petrol into the duct, for it would flow without relation to the passage of air, and flooding would ensue; instead, a float-chamber (similar to a miniature domestic water cistern) holds a supply of petrol at a level just below that of the orifice through which the petrol emerges into the air stream, and the suction suffices to draw it up and through the hole.

In this way, the flow of petrol obviously increases as the velocity of air flow (and hence the suction) increases. Unfortunately, the laws governing the flow of liquids are different from those for gases, so the two flow rates do not increase in direct proportion. This is the basic shortcoming of the simple spray carburettor: it can only work properly at one speed. Increase the engine speed and the flow of air through the venturi will increase in proportion (both in quantity and velocity), but the flow of petrol will increase more. The discrepancy is great enough to be serious: doubling the engine speed will enrich the mixture by about 25%, correspondingly, reducing the engine speed would weaken the mixture. Not only does this variability ruin all hopes of consistently accurate carburation, it also makes starting the engine virtually impossible without some additional means of enriching what would be an impossibly weak starting mixture, since no normal engine is capable of burning a petrol/air mixture weaker than about 1:21 by weight.

At a very early stage came additional complications: a throttle (a valve in the form of a hinged flap, a sliding plate, a

Above: an exploded diagram of an average carburettor showing the principal functions and components

Left: a cutaway drawing of an Amal Mark 2 carburettor which features an aluminium-alloy body, a concentrically tapering air-intake tube, a cold-start mixture-enriching lever, two float chamber vent tubes and a screw-top for easy access to the mixing chamber

revolving barrel, an intrusive plunger or some other device) was placed in the air duct to control the amount of air admitted, and thus regulate the performance of the engine, after earlier attempts to control it by altering the spark timing had been found inadequate. Thereafter, the complications proliferated as more and more anomalies were found in the behaviour of the basic carburettor. Spluttering when the throttle was suddenly opened proved to be due to the inertia of the petrol resisting prompt increase in flow rate, causing a temporary weakening of the mixture. Starting a cold engine was found to demand a mixture as rich as 1:2, and warming up thereafter needed about 1:5, despite the theoretical impossibility of burning such a rich dosage. In fact, not all the petrol was burned: the surplus was turned into carbon, and the exhaust was rich in carbon monoxide.

A related problem was found to be that of properly atomising the petrol in the air: large droplets have too much inertia and do not follow the path of the air flow into the cylinder – as was dramatically demonstrated by engineer Jack Williams during development work on the AJS 7R engine. A well atomised supply consists of the most minute droplets, each surrounded by a sphere of vapour much bigger than the droplet itself. Good vaporisation ensures ready inflammation and good combustion, but it also has a pronounced cooling effect which, although normally beneficially increasing the charge density, can lead to the carburettor becoming choked with ice when the atmosphere is cool and humid. Other problems were created more by the carburettor's working conditions than by its inherent failings. Unskilled or uneducated riders might not make proper use of mixture-enriching devices for starting, being particularly likely to leave them in operation too long. The longitudinal accelerations induced by accelerating or braking hard, and lateral accelerations when cornering sidecar outfits, would disturb the fuel level in the float chamber so much that the carburettor jet might be starved of petrol or flooded, causing the engine to cut-out briefly or even to stall when braking. Heat conducted from the cylinder head into the body of the carburettor might cause fuel to vaporise in the wrong place.

Worst of all was vibration, for which the motor cyclist has always displayed an inexplicably insensible tolerance that he expected his carburettor somehow to emulate. It is vibration as much as airborne dust that causes throttle slides to wear out so rapidly; it is vibration that not only hammers flow-check valve needles into their seats until they are deformed beyond hope of functioning efficiently, but also makes the fuel froth in the float chamber, to produce uncontrollable aberrations in mixture strength. The first effective cure for frothing was the remotely mounted float chamber devised by Amal for their GP racing carburettor, but the main body of the carburettor remained firmly fixed to the engine which was the source of most vibration. Only within the last decade has it become common practice to mount the carburettor on a flexible rubber extension of the inlet pipe, a technique pioneered in racing cars nearly thirty years ago.

Since the 1920s, or even before, the development of motor car carburettors diverged from established motor cycle practice. Only the occasional application of Amals to a competition car, as in the cases of the Dixon Rileys of the 1930s, or the Abingdon-prepared Minis and Midgets of the 1960s, served to suggest that if they could produce such prodigious performance, these deceptively simple instruments might have been unjustly ignored. Very often it was, literally, ignorance: there were many car engineers who could see no further than the fact that a motor cycle carburettor was operated by cable – which was once (and perhaps properly) considered neither dignified nor dependable. Today, however, car practice has crept into motor cycle engineering, and it is necessary to look at all kinds. From cars, we had two principle types, the constant-vacuum carburettor inspired by the SU and the fixed-venturi type of which the Weber (occasionally seen on sprint motor cycles) is a good example. Commercial considerations had more to do with their dominion than did their efficacy as carburettors, while their manufacturers preserved a singular obstinacy in refusing to recognise the virtues of rival kinds. Only in the early 1960s was a carburettor combining the characteristics of both put into production in Japan by Keihin for Honda cars, and this may be seen as the birth of the complex modern instrument. The constant-vacuum type is a simple one that is difficult to adjust, while the fixed-venturi type is complex in construction but easy to adjust. Put the two together and you have a complex carburettor that is hard to get right. In honourable contrast, the better class of motor cycle carburettor has all the subtlety of operation of a complex instrument while retaining (both in

Right: the major components of a carburettor; from the top – retaining ring, cable locator, spring, throttle slide and needle, carburettor body and float chamber bowl

Far right: three stages in the operation of a constant-vacuum carburettor; at tickover (left) the piston is almost completely down, while under running conditions (centre) piston/needle height varies with throttle opening, an oil damper delaying movement under acceleration; the 'choke' operates in this case by lowering the jet

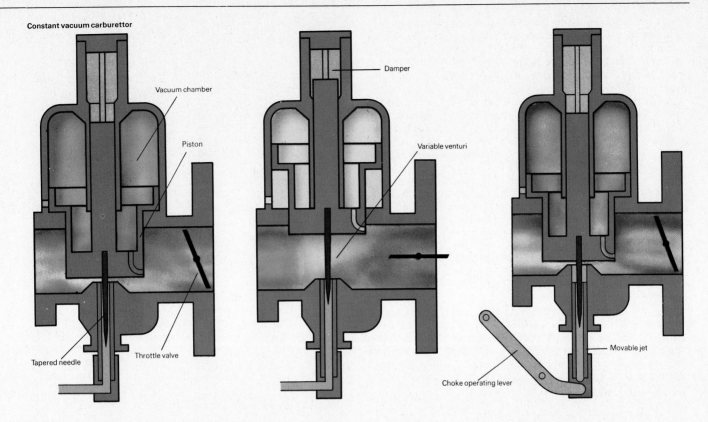

Constant vacuum carburettor

Vacuum chamber

Piston

Damper

Variable venturi

Tapered needle

Throttle valve

Choke operating lever

Movable jet

construction and in adjustment) all its simplicity.

The constant-vacuum carburettor, which has been tried in the past in such improbable surroundings as the Triumph Thunderbird, may be found today in certain Suzuki and BMW models. It has like all others a throttle valve, a venturi and a constant-level supply of petrol. Its special feature is the nature of its venturi, a constriction created by the obstruction of a slide (usually in the form of a piston) that is caused to rise and fall by the variations in partial vacuum of the inlet tract caused by throttle position and engine load. As the slide moves to obstruct the inlet passage more or less, it thus maintains a constant pressure drop across the petrol jet orifice. This, as we have seen, would not be enough to ensure the correct flow in all circumstances; but, by attaching to this slide a needle of varying cross section which moves in and out of the petrol discharge orifice, and thus alters the cross-sectional area of fuel flow, the necessary adjustments are made. Over its working range, the constant-vacuum carburettor thus gives a sensibly constant mixture strength under all conditions. Enrichment for starting can be contrived either by moving the jet downwards relative to the needle, or by strangling the intake. The slight enrichment needed for idling is procured by modifying the contours of the needle. For acceleration, the inertia of the slide is relied on (perhaps further slowed by a simple oil damper) to delay its opening, so increasing the pressure drop over the venturi and stimulating a stronger flow of petrol.

Ostensibly simple, the adjustments of this type of instrument demands subtle understanding of its working. Varying the weight of the slide, the rigour of its damping, the strength of the spring which tends to close the venturi and the thickness and contours of the needle, all produce changes which interact.

The fixed-venturi carburettor makes up in multiplicity of air and petrol passages what it lacks in variable geometry. Details vary enormously in different makes and models, but in principle the idea is to bring into action various supplementary petrol jets and air bleeds at various conjunctions of engine speed and load, each one serving to enrich or impoverish

the mixture as necessary. Apart from spring-loaded accelerator pumps which can be used to squirt extra petrol into the inlet tract when the throttles are opened for more power, most of the changes in air and fluid circuitry are effected by purely pneumatic means: when a particular jet is subjected to suction, fuel will flow from it until the suction is removed by a change in throttle position or air-flow velocity.

A good way to improve the flexibility of response of a fixed-venturi carburettor is to give it two air passages, each with its own throttle and its own particular set of jets. The throttles open progressively in succession, so that for gentle riding only the primary barrel will be used together with a variety of starting, pilot and other jets serving it. At full load, both throttles will be open, the secondary passage being served by a larger main jet. This compound carburettor is common in cars but rare in motor cycles, finding an unique place on the Wankel engine of the Suzuki RE5.

The classical motor cycle carburettor is a compound instrument, too, but is not usually recognised as such. Over most of its working range, it is controlled by a slide (usually of piston-like formation) which may be raised progressively to vary the cross-sectional area of the venturi, carrying with it a tapered needle which correspondingly increases the fuel flow. Progressive correction is applied by a supplementary air passage that leads to a chamber surrounding the submerged spray jet, air thus introduced mixing with the fuel to form an emulsion that reduces fuel flow in conditions where it would otherwise be excessive.

The idle circuit is similar, its air coming from another supplementary passage. However, it works in conditions where the throttle is closed, with the slide dropped right down against its stop and almost completely closing the main air passage. In these circumstances, the air burrows through the idling circuit underneath, collecting fuel to form an emulsion that emerges from a tiny main air passage downstream of the throttle slide. This subsystem works rather like a fixed-venturi carburettor, the pneumatic conditions that make it work being destroyed when the throttle valve is raised, so as to destroy the vacuum over the idle orifice further downstream. The important but often overlooked secret of the motor cycle carburettor then comes into play: the bottom of the throttle slide is fairly deeply recessed, with a cut-away at the leading edge which may be adjusted (by substitution of slides) to modify the vacuum created underneath the slide when the throttle is moving upwards. This vacuum causes an enrichment of the mixture, giving all the performance characteristics of an accelerator pump without any mechanical complications.

Alas, such complications cannot now be avoided, and this fundamentally simple apparatus is corrupted by modern refinements. Mixture-enriching devices for starting (commonly called 'chokes' even though they are often supplementary fuel supplies rather than air stranglers) are sometimes made automatic, responding by thermostatic control to the temperature of the engine. Vaporisation of fuel from the float-chamber is no longer allowed to escape into the atmosphere in countries where strict laws against the emission of unburned hydrocarbons are in force, but has to be piped to some form of condenser and returned to the fuel tank, or failing that is led to the plenum chamber from which the carburettor draws filtered and silenced air. Other automatic devices such as spring-loaded flaps in the throttle plate or strangler admit extra air when the engine is running at high speed with closed throttle, weakening what would otherwise be too rich a mixture such as might lead to an unsociably foul exhaust. Perhaps if this sophistry continues, we will end up with petrol injection apparatus after all.   LJKS

Above: one of the two Bing constant-vacuum carburettors on BMW R100RS

Below: one of the Dell'Orto carburettors on the Moto Guzzi 850 Le Mans

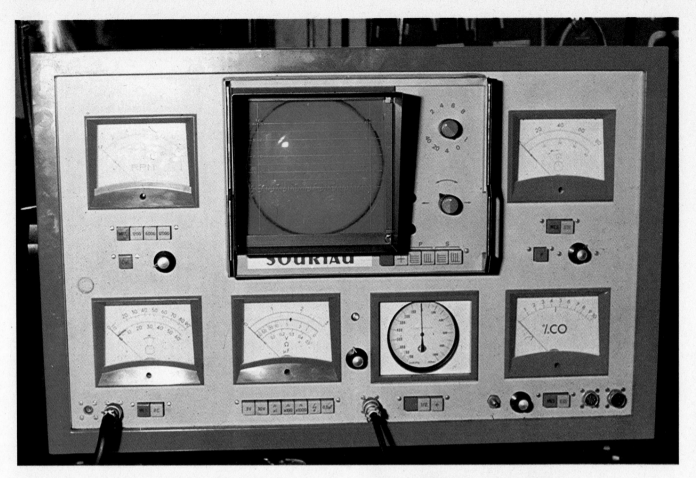

IF POSSIBLE, A COMPRESSION check should be made as the first step, to ensure that the valves and bores of the engine are all in good condition. A low reading on one cylinder will make all attempts at obtaining a smooth idle a waste of time. The spark plugs should be cleaned and gapped and, on a two stroke, the exhaust system should be checked to make sure that it is thoroughly devoid of carbon build up. It is also important to check that the air filter is clean. As the filter will be disconnected during the tuning operation it will not affect the running until it is reconnected and the bike is ridden away. A dirty filter will cancel out all the time and effort that has been put into setting up the carbs.

While you would not expect a TV repair man to attack the back of your set with an axe it is possible for an experienced man to set up a four carburettor engine with a screwdriver, four lollipop sticks and a lump of rubber hose. To be more realistic, at least one vacuum gauge will probably be needed alongside your lolly sticks and screwdriver. Before going into any details of how to set up a carburettor it is necessary to consider exactly what is the object of the adjustments and what settings have been predetermined by the makers of a particular machine. With a single carburettor engine, the only adjustments that can be made are to the idle system. There are two screws to set, one altering the actual mixture ratio of the petrol and air that the engine digests on idle and the other determining the speed at which the motor ticks over. The adjustment of a single carburettor is extremely simple. The mixture screw should be altered until the engine ticks over smoothly, consistent with a clean pick up as the throttle is opened. It may be found that after adjusting the mixture screw to its optimum position the idle speed will be too high. The throttle stop screw is therefore used to determine the speed of idle. The rest of the settings will have been pre-determined by the manufacturer when the engine was developed. That, however, is not the end of the story because,

Adjusting the Mixture

To the inexperienced, adjusting carburettors can be great fun. The novice whose bike has four carburettors can spend many happy hours tinkering with mixture screws, checking vacuum gauge readings and playing with the balance screws, all in a futile attempt to eliminate a rough idle which is being caused by a faulty spark plug! Before even attempting to adjust the carbs on an engine it should be ensured that the rest of the unit is in otherwise perfect tune.

like people, no two engine units can ever be exactly the same. Due to production tolerances some engines come off the line much tighter than others, yet they are all fitted with the same carburettors, which in themselves can vary as to the mixture ratios that they will dispense, despite being fitted with the same jets and slides. It is partly for these reasons that two otherwise identical engines can give vastly different power outputs. It is possible therefore to tailor the carburation to suit the individual engine provided access to sophisticated equip-

Above: electronic engine tuning apparatus incorporating exhaust gas analyser, ignition oscilloscope, dwell meter, tachometer and vacuum gauge

which screw does what. There is no point in adjusting the 'mixture' screw only to find it draining the float bowl. A handbook or manual will show which screw is which. The mixture screw should first be set to its standard position as given in the handbook. This will be around one to two turns out from fully home depending on the make of carb. It should be noted that fully home does *not* mean that the screw should be tightened with the biggest driver to be found. Excessive force on the mixture screw will certainly damage the taper and may even scrap the carb by breaking the body at the pilot drilling. Having set the mixture screws, the next operation is to adjust the throttle stops, or idle screws as they are often referred to. For this operation one or more vacuum gauges will be needed, or a piece of rubber tube and one very experienced ear that can tell a carb intake hiss from a rear wheel puncture. As few people have the experience or confidence to work by ear, use of a vacuum gauge, or gauges becomes necessary and these will have to be damped out. Quite simply this means that the take off for the gauge needs a restriction, or small hole in it, to damp out the fluctuations in the vacuum which occur as the inlet valve opens and closes. A single gauge can be effectively damped out by clamping the take off rubber tube until the gauge needle is steady enough to read. It should be remembered that the steadier the needle is, the less sensitive it is to smaller variations in pressure and some compromise is necessary.

After starting the engine the gauge is connected to each intake in turn and the throttle stop adjusted until the same reading is obtained for each carb. Once the carburettors are thus balanced the idle speed is adjusted by altering each screw by the same amount and then the balance is rechecked.

The fine tuning of the mixture screws can, in theory be carried out by altering the mixture screw to give the highest reading on the vacuum gauge but in practice the needles are rarely steady enough. A more reliable method is to alter each of the screws by the same amount, within one half a turn of the standard setting, until the engine runs smoothly. A method that is often recommended for setting up the mixture of twin carbs is to stop the spark to one cylinder and tune the remaining one as for a single, then repeat for the other side. The problem with this method is that the carburettor being tuned is only being set to its optimum position when the second cylinder is acting as a passenger. This means that with both

ment such as an engine brake is available. Problems again arise because most carburettors are mass produced and consequently many of their characteristics are predetermined by the form of air corrector drillings; these cannot readily be altered. For this reason it is not usually feasible to transfer carbs from one machine to another, even though they may look alike and have the same choke size. Although it is possible to obtain a carburettor that can be adjusted by means of chokes and jets to suit any engine, the cost of such instruments prohibits their use on mass produced motor cycles.

Owners of large capacity, multi-carbed motor cycles can gain the impression that carburettor tuning will only affect the idle, and be reluctant to attempt any adjustment. In practice, a powerful bike will cruise on the open road with the throttle only open to about one eighth of its full travel and at this setting the idle mixture is still contributing significantly to the carburation. For this very reason an engine with the idle mixtures poorly set will use more fuel when cruising than one properly set up. Well-balanced carburettors will also contribute to the physical long life of the engine as all the cylinders will be pulling together instead of working against each other.

Having established that carburettor adjustment is worthwhile we can now take a look at the procedure. As has already been stated it should be ensured that the engine is worth tuning before work is started and also that it has reached its correct operating temperature. Nothing is more frustrating than setting up the carbs only to find that your settings 'go out' after a short run because the engine was not really hot enough when the work was done.

Assuming the carburettors are badly out of tune, the first step is to loosen off the linkages or cables to check that they are not holding the throttles open. The next step is to determine

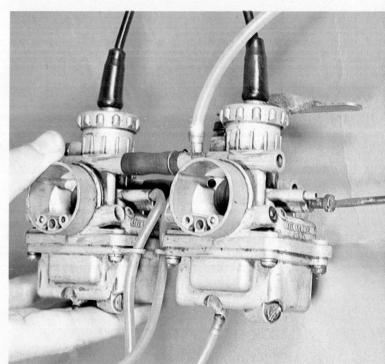

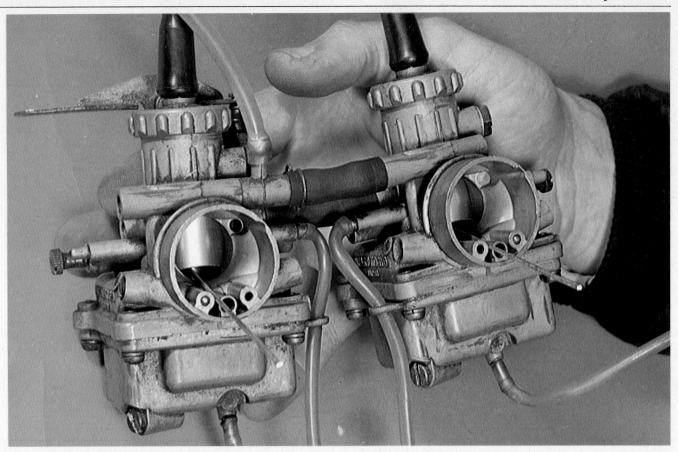

Far left: the finger points to the throttle cable adjuster

Below left: adjusting the mixture screw with a screwdriver

Above: balancing twin carburettors using two pieces of wire (lollypop sticks would do). As the throttle is opened, so the sticks will move, indicating balanced or unbalanced carburettors

cylinders firing, the idle mixture is no longer correct.

On the subject of balancing, we have previously mentioned the use of a rubber tube and this, literally, coupled to an experienced ear, can be used to set up the balance but not the mixture. The idea is that one end of the tube is held to the ear and the other end is put up against the carburettor intake, with the air filters removed. The intake hiss can then be listened to. By adjusting the stops until all the carbs are 'hissing' with the same note the same result can be achieved as with the vacuum gauge system. Alternatively carb balancers are available which are held over the intake to measure the intake air speed. They tend not to be as accurate as the traditional vacuum gauge.

At this stage the engine should be ticking over quite nicely but will probably still not pick up cleanly. This problem will disappear once the throttle rods or cables have been balanced. The basic idea is to have some free play in the operating linkage so that the throttle slides are always free to rest on their respective stops but they must also all lift at the same time. If they do not all lift together then some of the cylinders will try to lead the others and in fact will always be trying to do more than their fair share of work, so the engine will run roughly as it is no longer in balance.

It is at this stage that we can introduce our lollipop sticks! By tucking a short length of rod under each slide, so that it is just visible in the bellmouth, it should be possible to see the slides move as the throttle is operated. The linkages can then

be adjusted until the rods all begin to move at the same time. When fitting the rods it should be ensured that the slides are not being lifted off their stops, which would be defeating the object of the exercise. An alternative method, given sufficient access, is simply to look down the throats' of the carbs and note which slides are opening late.

The foregoing relates to fixed jet and Amal type carburettors but there are other types of carburettor which have no throttle stop screws. This is usually the case on fairly new bikes fitted with constant vacuum carbs, a type which BMW have used for some time. With this type of carburettor the air slide is replaced by a butterfly, as on most cars. Once these are balanced at tickover they remain correct, as the twistgrip is normally only connected to one carb and this operates the others. The BMW, of course, because of its engine layout still demands the use of separate cables. On most bikes the balance is determined by having the butterflys linked via a spring loaded clamp which is adjustable via a small screw. Altering this screw changes the butterfly position in relation to it's neighbour. Once the carburettors are in balance the overall engine speed is set normally by a knurled screw arrangement. This is fine if the carburettors are mounted next to each other as on a straight four engine but the BMW has to have one carb on either side of the engine and linking them with a two foot rod is not practicable. BMW have stuck to cables for this reason.

Cable adjustment is one aspect of carburettor adjustment that is often overlooked. Apart from being regularly checked for signs of impending failure, the cable or cables should also be checked for adjustment after setting up the carbs. Some free play at the twistgrip should be allowed or the cable may be doing the job of the throttle stops and causing an uneven tickover. Many modern machines are now fitted with a closing cable which should also have its fair share of free play. If the closing cable on some machines is over adjusted it can actually bend the linkages and then major problems will arise in getting the carburettors to balance.   VM

'EASTERN' BIKES FROM PORTUGAL

Look in the showrooms of any major motor cycle dealer, and there, nestling among the Japanese lightweights you will almost certainly see one or two Casals. Although styled as if they come from the land of the rising sun, they do in fact come from a relatively small town in Portugal called Aveiro.

Portugal has never had a reputation for building mopeds or motor cycles and, in past years, tended to be overlooked. However, things are changing, and there is a thriving industry there. The main companies are SIS and Casal, although there are some more of smaller size. While SIS manufacture lightweights of 50cc with imported Sachs motors, Casal produce their own engines and cycle components. In a way, the Casal story could be likened to Honda, although it is on a much smaller scale and not quite so rapid.

Portugal not being one of the wealthiest of countries, relatively cheap and economical transportation has been a must for a good many years. The climate is, of course, very agreeable to two-wheeled travel, so there are two good basic reasons for the creation and growth of a moped and motor cycle industry.

Strangely enough, though, Casal did not set out, initially, to make motor cycles. Señor J. Casal formed his company, Metalurgia Casal in 1953, to produce engines. These were for agricultural and industrial use primarily, but some were also made for various other factories to install in their mopeds and light motor cycles. Looking at the smaller Casal engines of today, you will notice that the crankcases at least resemble those of the large West German Zündapp company. Not a surprise when you know that when Señor Casal formed his company, he enlisted the aid of Zündapp who supplied technicians who stayed with the company until as recently as 1971. All the Casal engines produced to date have been of two-stroke design, although this might change in the future.

Building his new factory in 1953 in Aveiro, a town of some 30,000 people, Señor Casal soon found a good reliable home market to absorb his production. A great asset this, for it is well known that a good local market is an asset when a factory has thoughts about exportation in any form. In fact, Casal, even today, sell around 80% of their production in Portugal! The engines, most of them fan-cooled, sold well, and it was 1964 before the first actual Casal vehicle was produced, it was in fact a motor scooter. Named the Karina S170, it was a 50cc two-stroke with an output of 5.2bhp at 7500rpm. The rear chain ran in an oilbath, and it was a model that proved popular. The year 1967 was when the first true Casal moped came on to the scene, the two-speed K160. Quite

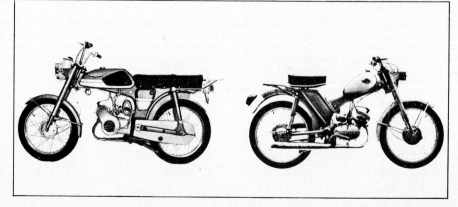

ordinary, as mopeds go, it was soon accompanied by the K161, the latter having footrests and a kickstarter. In the midst of this, the factory changed its name to Metalurgia Casal Sarl becoming a joint-stock company. The mopeds proved to be as popular as the scooter and the engine units before them and, for many years, the factory achieved production increases of 30% per annum. No slight achievement.

Opposite page, top: the Casal M131, a 50cc engine for industrial applications

Bottom left: the K190 Casal tourer produced 5.3bhp at 7500rpm. This 50cc machine has a four-speed gearbox

Bottom right: Casal's K161 of 1957 was fitted with footrests and a kickstart, making it, in effect, the first Casal motor cycle

This page, below left: the Casal S2 Commuter Sport model, a two-speed bike, with hand-change of 2.5bhp

Bottom left: the SS4 Super Sports, developing 5.3bhp at 7500rpm from 50cc

Below: the K270, 125cc two stroke and the 250cc K280 of 1975, which is fitted with a front-wheel disc brake

When, in 1970, it was agreed that the Casal factory should become independent of the West German advisers, it was necessary to recruit young engineers from Portuguese universities. The change in personnel coincided with the company's evaluation of the current situation and how the company should direct its efforts in the future. The Japanese were obviously the people to try to match, and the engineers looked carefully at the types of machines they made and sold in such great volume. First, a new 125cc touring motor cycle was introduced, the K260. Very good looking, it featured a pressed-steel frame, five gears, and produced 12bhp at 7000rpm. Undoubtedly, the production of this machine demonstrated that the Portuguese had learned much from their tutors, and could turn out some real quality machinery themselves. After so much rapid expansion, the company was already starting to take a serious interest in exporting, the first mopeds went to Denmark in fact, in 1968, but now other larger markets were to come under attack. A branch of the factory was soon opened in Angola, which is intended to supply the markets of southern Africa, and other countries were soon to be supplied direct from Aveiro.

The 50cc class, and the 75cc, too, took up a great deal of Casal time in the early 1970s, for these were the classes that Casal reckoned they would have most success in. A whole host of these capacity machines rolled out of the factory gates in the ensuing years: pure tourers with footrests, fan-cooled engines and fully enclosed rear chains; sporty models to attract the youngsters; and even little trail bikes. Many had a definite oriental look about them, and this was a wise move. The public buying the smaller capacity machines were attracted to this conception, with such massive advertising from Japanese manufacturers, and Casal benefited by it. In no way did Casal copy the Japanese, but merely followed their general styling ideas, and they looked good.

More sporting 125cc motor cycles were produced, the K270 being of most interest. The engine, very much the same as that fitted to the K260, being suspended beneath the duplex frame tubes that ran down and over the top of the crankcase. Very attractive to the youngsters, the K270 eventually sprouted a front disc brake and a very racy image overall. While most of the production was still mopeds and slightly larger motor cycles, the development of bigger bikes continued. A 125cc motocross machine was said to be under test, but

Above: the K260 of 1971 was the first new model to come out of the factory after the intake of Portuguese personnel

Bottom left and centre: two views of the Casal Phantom 5, a five-speed foot-change sports moped of 50cc, producing 6.2bhp at 7500rpm. The Phantom is fitted with twin leading shoe brakes front and rear

had not appeared by late 1976. What did show up in 1975, however, was a brand new 250cc sports tourer, the K280. Entirely new, the engine included, it was a very attractive machine. A two-stroke in the best Casal tradition, it had a long megaphone exhaust system and a sturdy front disc brake. Not yet seen outside Portugal in any quantity, it is likely that Casal are putting some more of their ideas into it. Certainly, it promises to be an excellent machine.

There are reports that 350 and 500cc Casals are under development, and these, breaking completely with those traditions just mentioned, are apparently of four-strokes design.

Just like Honda, the Casal factory wants to become involved in the production of cars, too, and in fact there are, in 1976, moves afoot already to this end.

Señor Casal could not, surely, have dreamed how his new factory was going to expand: new buildings have been added through the years; they cover more than seventeen and a half thousand square metres and are still growing! The workforce has increased too, and is more than a thousand strong. There is no slackening of the pace, and it seems that Casal is going to be a much bigger name in the future. Indeed, 'Produce of Portugal' could soon be more widely used when referring to Casals than to the famous wine! DJ

If an Englishman was to look for a little piece of Britain in California, then certainly the place he should head for are the counties surrounding San Francisco. Affectionately known throughout California as the 'Bay Area', this northern region boasts of hills covered with lush green trees and vegetation, the likes of which hot and dry southern California can only dream of. Considering the climate, one might suspect that motor cycle racing would be more popular in the south than in the north, but this is not necessarily so. The Bay Area is a hotbed of motor cycling activity and in the past has produced such great American racers as Mert Lawwill, Mark Brelsford and Kenny Roberts.

Don Castro also came from the Bay Area: he was born and raised in Hollister, south of San Francisco in an area the locals proudly call the artichoke centre of the World. Although he was small, Don was quite athletic, excelling in football, baseball and basketball. Considering the area, it was not surprising that his favourite hobbies were hunting and fishing but, at the age of sixteen, he discovered yet a third love, motor cycle racing.

Actually, Don was introduced to the world of speed at the age of nine on a kart, but it was not until motor cycles came along that he considered racing professionally. After two years of riding local scrambles, Don applied for and received his professional racing licence. By the end of the year, he was fifth in the AMA National Novice Championship.

The American Motor cyclist Association's racer grading system requires that a rider spend one full year racing in the Novice division and one year in the Junior division before promotion to 'expert'. Advancement depends on gathering a certain number of points in each grade.

Don easily advanced to Junior; in fact, he would have won the Junior National Championship in 1969 if it were not for flamboyant and spectacular David Aldana. David had a reputation for riding much faster than his experience was ready for. Although Aldana won the championship, Castro served notice by winning six National Junior races. At one event, the Sacramento mile dirt race, his Junior qualifying time was faster than all Experts except one. The following year, at the age of twenty, Don Castro made the Expert grade.

The Triumph factory was quick to enlist Don into their 1970 racing team. This was the year the team first raced the fabulous three-cylinder 750cc roadracers. Although Don had road raced only twice before, he was given

Right: Don Castro from Hollister, California

Below: at Mallory Park, Leicestershire, during the 1975 Transatlantic series, on a 750 Yamaha

Opposite page: riding for Triumph in the first Anglo-American series, during 1971, and doing a startline interview at Mallory Park during a lull in the action

the opportunity to ride one of the triples. He finished third at Daytona, the most important race of the year. It was the beginning of an excellent year for Don: riding factory dirt trackers and road racers, he finished his rookie Expert season as the fifth ranked rider in the championships.

In 1971, Don's Triumph contract was renewed, and he finished ninth at Daytona and was selected for the Anglo American Match Race Team. His highest finish at the Match Race Series was a third at Brands Hatch behind Ray Pickrell and Paul Smart. In the American National Championships, he did not fare as well as the previous year and he finished the season as the ninth ranked rider.

Triumph did not renew Don's contract for 1972, as budget cut-backs had reduced the team to only two riders, National Champion Dick Mann and former champion Gene Romero. The role of privateer did not suit Don Castro. There was the occasional high finish, but machinery problems frequently prevented him from scoring points. That all-important first National win still eluded him and, by the end of the season, he had slipped to twelfth place in the National Championship. Yamaha, however, had not forgotten the talented youngster and just when things looked grim Don was offered a full factory contract for 1973.

Together with team-mates Kenny Roberts, Gene Romero and Kel

Carruthers, the Yamaha Team took the National Circuit by storm. At Daytona, Don proved that his road racing had not suffered since the Triumph days by taking second in the 250 race. Forced to ride a 350 in the 750 class he finished ninth in the Daytona 200, sixth at Charlotte, sixth at Dallas and fourth at Talladega. More importantly, his dirt-track results were high as well and he finally won that first ever National race, a half-mile event at San Jose. By the end of the year, Don's name was once again high on the Championship list: he was fifth.

1974 could have been Don Castro's finest year. At Daytona, he startled favourite Kenny Roberts by winning the 250 race. In the 200 mile event, Yamaha entered their new 700cc four and Don took fourth place. Sadly, shortly after Daytona, a crash in a dirt race spelled the turning point in Don's racing career. Another American racer, Cal Rayborn had died in a road race in New Zealand, and it was in his memory that a Cal Rayborn Memorial Benefit race was being held in Chula Vista, California. The Harley Davidson Team, of which Cal was a life-long member, did not even bother to send any team riders to the non-championship event. Don Castro went, however, on his factory Yamaha.

The crash tore the ligaments in Don's left leg and forced him to miss half of the season including the Anglo American Match Races. When he

BAY CITY RACER

returned to racing four months later, he finished third at the Laguna Seca 250cc Roadrace but had to withdraw from riding the big bike event due to pain in his still-healing leg. By the time Talladega rolled around, he was back in the groove and finished second. Then at Ontario while lying second and lapping a slower rider, Don came off at 120mph. Although he walked away from the crash, it did not leave him unaffected. His weak leg had prevented him from doing many dirt races and, as a result, by the end of the year Don's name was very low indeed on the Championship list.

Just as had happened during the Triumph factory days, budget cut backs forced Yamaha to release Don from his contract in 1975, although he was still asked to ride three road races. Reduced once more to the role of privateer, Don did not do much dirt racing that year. On occasion he would show up at a National on an oddball machine such as a three-cylinder Kawasaki dirt tracker. It was obvious, however, that his heart was not in it. His road race performances were poor as well and on his very last ride on a factory machine he was forced to retire at Ontario due to heat prostration. At the end of the year, his name was nowhere to be seen in the National Ratings at all.

There are numerous stories of promising young racers who seem destined to reach the top only to fade into obscurity. Why Don's career floundered only he knows. Perhaps it was his inability to adapt to privateer racing after his years on factory teams. Perhaps his greatest misfortune was that on those teams he was always overshadowed by more flamboyant team members, the spectacular David Aldana, colourful Gene Romero and super-star, twice National Champion Kenny Roberts. Quiet, unassuming, friendly and likable, Don was one of the most non-controversial riders around. That he had talent was undeniable, two National wins proved it. But even those two wins appeared to not give him the recognition he needed.

Or perhaps it was the painful crash in 1974 that convinced Don that racing was not for him. He did not have to attend that non-championship race in Cula Vista, but he wanted to pay his respects to fallen comrade Cal Rayborn: Don Castro was that kind of man. It was not until late in 1976 that Don's name finally reappeared in the Motorcycling papers. 'Don Castro, 27, ex-factory motorcycle racer for Triumph and Yamaha and winner of two National Championship races has announced his retirement from the sport'.

FV

PHOENIX
OF THE NORTH

I n 1971, the world of motor cycling received the saddening news that BSA were closing their competition shop and disbanding their six-man motocross team. It was regrettable because it was the closing chapter of a company which had brought England some of its finest moments in scrambling and which had nurtured some of Britain's best riders. Indeed, it could be said that the one of the greatest British riders of all, Jeff Smith, came from that Birmingham firm. There was something else which many felt unhappy about at the end of that year, too. With the disappearance of the BSA, it was thought that it was the end of the four-stroke engine in moto-cross, and that the last bastion had fallen.

What was not known was that a young man from Bolton had taken the journey to Small Heath to see about buying a couple of frames. He had heard that, since the competition shop had closed, many unused parts were lying idle and he had a use for two frames at least. 'When I got there, I saw Brian Martin the ex-Competition Manager. He said that he could not let me have just a couple of frames but, if I was interested, I could buy the lot. Now that amounted to twelve frames, some wheels and front forks. It was more than I wanted really but I decided to take them back to Bolton. I made up a bike using these bits and a BSA engine; a chap showed interest in

Left: Bob Wright gets airborne on a 500 CCM

Right: Norman Barrow on 500 CCM at a meeting at Halstead, Essex

Below: the 1974 500cc CCM model

it so I sold it to him. So, I made another more or less the same, a buyer came along and I sold that one, and from there things have just grown.' The man who went to BSA was Alan Clews and from the ashes of that once great company came CCM: Clews Competition Machines.

If you ever go to a motocross meeting and find the CCM camp you may have difficulty picking out the man in charge, because he is a rather shy man with a phlegmatic temperament. In fact, you would not be blamed for mistaking him for a spectator such is his coolness. Of course, there is nothing sluggish about someone who has taken a few remnants and turned it into a thriving company in one of the most unpredictable fields of business: that of the British motor cycle industry. He has, in the short time he has been in the trade, doubled the turnover of his company and is now in the £250,000 a year bracket. CCM have done well in the export market: in 1975, they increased their export business by 47% which, in monetary terms, is £55,000; the following year, 1976, they had shown an increase of 62% (£116,000).

Born in 1938 at Toddington, a village near Bury, Clews has lived all his life in the North. After he left school, he took a job with Avery repairing, weighting and testing machines. 'I found this could do a lot for you because I used to go around the factories in the Bolton and Manchester area and I got the opportunity to see how different things were made'. At that time, he was studying at the local evening classes and finally reached Ordinary National Certificate level in both mechanical and electrical engineering. He comes from a poor background so expensive hobbies were not welcomed at home. Nevertheless, he managed to find himself a bike when he was sixteen and did a little trials riding. It was not until he was 24 that he got seriously involved as a rider in motocross, however. 'I bought a Rickman frame kit and entered the open-to-centre meetings. I had this great big crash helmet and, when I was racing, my head used to bob about inside the thing', he said. Although he never became a champion, he reached international level and rode in France, West Germany and Switzerland.

Originally, Alan called his own machines Clewstrokes but changed it to CCM in 1973 when he bought a batch of B50s from BSA. 'These were virtually GP models, very light, and I think the plan was to send them to 24 dealers in America as a promotion but it never got that far. I had some B44s before these came along. They were the 441cc models.' Clews set out on his adventure with a few bikes from a company going into liquidation; a source soon to dry up. He then bought a new factory which he moved into in 1976; it covered nearly

Above: Britain's Eddie Kidd, jumping thirteen buses on a CCM in 1976

Top left: James Aird on CCM, 1976

Below left: Vic Eastwood on his CCM at the Tweedledown scramble, 1976

16,000 square feet. He bought fifty machine tools from the old BSA factory at Small Heath to make the B50. In addition to that equipment, Clews bought all the jigs, dies and drawings and all the raw materials from BSA so he could carry on making the CCM for as long as he wanted.

Initially, the company was no more than three people strong, but between them they made 39 motor cycles. In 1973, they put together 150 machines and the next year this had risen to 160. 1975 saw a slight decrease with only 140 units completed but by the end of 1976 the figure was back up around the 170/180 mark. His list of employees now totals fifteen with a production manager, a workshop manager, two turners, two engine builders, welders, fabricators and motor cycle assemblers. The machines made go to America, Sweden, Holland, France, West Germany, Australia, Switzerland and Denmark; the rest are sold in England. Actually, the bikes amount to less than 50% of production, and it is with spares that the company keeps busy.

259

CCM have a team of works sponsored riders which includes such names as John Banks, Vic Eastwood and Vic Allan. It is incredible that a company so small can afford to give so much backing to the sport, which costs them £24,000. The CCMs for these riders were 500cc machines (there is a 600cc model). The engine is a four-stroke, single-cylinder type with the gearbox *en bloc*. A bore and stroke of 84mm × 90mm gives a capacity of 498cc and it produces 45bhp at 6500rpm.

Its compression ratio is 10.24:1 and, to keep the motor running smoothly, a full-flow oil system is adopted with the reservoir in the frame, which is made of T45 light-gauge tubing. This is the motor cycle which, at the moment, is the mainstay of Clews Competition Machines but there are plans for an Enduro model, a road bike and also a revolutionary five-stroke machine! Thus the phoenix of the north is now in flight.   RB

Right: the 500cc CCM stands ready for action

Below: the CCM has a full-flow oil system, incorporating its reservoir in the frame. The machine produces a workmanlike 45bhp

World Champion Teenager

Second place in a world championship is no mean achievement, particularly if the sport in question is enjoying an unprecedented boom, and the contestant is but a stripling youth of twenty years competing against much older and more experienced men. Yet, for Venezuelan rider Johnny Cecotto, 1976 was labelled a year of failure. Britain's Barry Sheene took some ten years to secure finally the coveted 500cc crown, yet Cecotto's second place in the 350cc championship came after just five years racing experience, and only three at top class level. The explanation lies in the astonishing fact that, just

Right: Johnny Cecotto from Venezuela took the 1975 World Championship for 350cc machines when aged nineteen

twelve months before, an even younger and more inexperienced Cecotto had carried off the 350 title at his first attempt, and had achieved a creditable fourth in the 250 class.

One year later, while undertaking the more ambitious task of capturing the 500cc title, he came unstuck in the process affecting his chances of retaining the 350cc title. No one likes a loser, and the newspaper headlines that had earlier proclaimed 'Cecotto King!' now demanded to know what had gone wrong. Critics formerly quick to praise now spoke of his inexperience, his fiery Latin temperament, his playboy life and dubbed him a 'nine day' wonder.

Cecotto was born on 25 January 1956 in Caracas and, although christened Alberto, somehow became known as Johnny. Like his English friend and counterpart, Barry Sheene, Johnny was born into a motor cycling family – his Italian born father, Giovanni, was a former Venezuelan champion on a Norton 500. Needless to say, there was little doubt that Johnny would eventually follow in his father's footsteps

. . . although perhaps few people at that time would have guessed the implications of that fateful day in 1971 when Johnny received a present from his father of a 750 Honda.

Lying about his age in order to race, Cecotto had competed in only two events when he was approached, first by the local Kawasaki importers, then shortly afterwards by Andres Ippolito, the wealthy and powerful importer of Yamaha motorcycles. To describe Cecotto's subsequent rise to stardom as mercurial would perhaps be an understatement. Despite his lack of racing experience, Johnny quickly emulated his father in 1974 by winning the Venezuelan championship for his Yamaha sponsors, followed shortly afterwards by the Latin American title. Still in 1974, European fans had their first glimpse of the fast rising star although, not surprisingly perhaps, his first outings were generally uninspiring as he struggled to get to grips with the demanding European circuits. Certainly, there was little indication of the bombshell about to burst on the

racing scene in 1975.

In the 1975 350cc championship, previously held by Agostini for no less than seven successive years, Cecotto was in shattering form and Ago could not match him. With four firsts, a second and a fifth place, Johnny took the title from the Italian maestro by no less than nineteen points. Not content with causing mayhem in the 350 class, he also raced to two firsts and two seconds to finish fourth in the 250cc class.

A foretaste of what was in store for European fans came in the opening round of the Championship in France. At the Paul Ricard circuit at Le Castellet, Cecotto powered his way to decisive victories in both the 250 and the 350 events, in each case setting new lap records. In the prestigious Daytona 200 in the USA, Cecotto, still a complete unknown outside his native Latin America, caused a sensation by turning in the third fastest lap time in practice and repeated a fine performance in the race proper.

Not that the season was a complete

Left: Cecotto at speed on his 500 Yamaha at Monza during the 1976 Italian Grand Prix

Below: although tempted by the glamour of motor racing, Johnny Cecotto could, with dedication, become a regular world beater on two wheels

success for, as with most top class riders, Cecotto had his fair share of spills. Yet not even high speed tumbles in Spain, Germany and Austria could stop the phenomenal progress of the nineteen year old rider who was now hitting the headlines in a big way. That year, Johnny Cecotto finally captured the 350 crown, curiously enough whilst sitting on a pit wall. With just two rounds to go, his arch rival Agostini needed to win the Czech Grand Prix to stay in the running. But in the fifth lap of the Brno course, Ago was forced to retire and, even though Cecotto himself had to pull out with mechanical problems, he limped back to the pits a world champion.

1976 began promisingly enough with full Yamaha support in both the 350 and 500 classes, but Cecotto returned first for another crack at Daytona. Despite finishing with an almost bald back tyre, he became the youngest ever rider to win the forty year old classic. Back in Europe, Cecotto again had good performances in France, Austria and Italy. However, the bubble had to burst sometime, and there then followed a succession of outings dogged by bad luck. With most of Yamaha's efforts channelled into Steve Baker's new 750 OW-31, their 500 mount proved to be no match for the all conquering Suzukis.

Cecotto was clearly unhappy and affairs came to a head in Holland when he even refused to practice on the factory 500 or travel to the Belgium Grand Prix the following week. In the 350 class, too, he seemed unable to recapture his winning form, and was forced to watch his early lead slowly whittled away by the Harley-Davidson rider Walter Villa. Despite a late challenge at the end of the season, it was Villa who eventually took the 350 title.

With an angry Cecotto threatening to quit two wheels for four, it seemed as though the motor cycle world was in danger of losing one of its brightest stars. However, although he admits to being tempted by the glamour of motor racing, it seems as though he will stick with Yamaha for the 350, 500 and the 750 championships. If his temper holds together and the new Yamahas are as quick as promised, there is no knowing how many races (or championships!) he might win in 1977.   SH

THE TRANSMISSION'S LINK

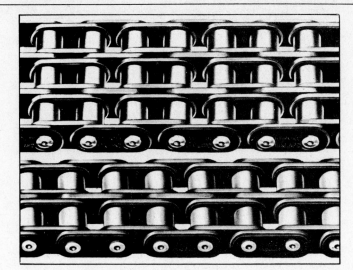

Above left: for reduced wear and increased power handling capacity, double-row (duplex) or even three-row (triplex) roller chains are needed

Left: the primary drive chain, a single-row roller unit, of an AJS single of the 1950s

Above: the secondary chain of the Zundapp 'GS' 125, complete with a full-length cover and adjusters on the rear wheel, with which to carry out chain tensioning

FOR WELL OVER FIFTY YEARS, chains have been widely used on motor cycles. In transmission systems, they ousted V-belts which had the advantages of quietness and resilience but, being inherently non-positive in their driving characteristics, were liable to slip under heavy load, especially if they were wet or had become worn, as they did rather frequently.

In contrast, the chain and its toothed sprockets provided a positive, efficient drive and lasted quite well even in adverse conditions. The roller chain was long virtually the only type used on motor cycles, but in one duty there has recently been something of a challenge from the inverted-tooth variety.

Few of today's motor cycles are chainless: the big majority have chain secondary drive between gearbox and rear wheel, and many also have a primary chain from engine to gearbox. In the days of separate magnetos and dynamos, these ancillaries were often driven by light chains, and for many years chains have also been favoured for driving overhead camshafts.

The precision roller chain was patented in 1880 by Hans Renold, a Swiss engineer who came to Britain to form his own manufacturing company which is still in the forefront nearly one hundred years later. The chain is built up of alternate inner and outer links; an inner link consists of two side plates connected by bushes carrying the rollers which give the chain its name and the rollers mesh with the sprocket teeth to give minimal running friction.

Each outer link comprises two more side plates bridged by bearing pins which run in the bushes of the adjacent inner links. The ends of the chain are preferably united, to make a continuous length, by riveting-up a connecting outer link. To facilitate fitting and removal, however, motor cycle rear chains are generally supplied 'open-ended', with a loose connecting link secured by a spring clip.

Roller chains are made in a number of standard pitches (pitch = nominal distance between successive bearing pins) and with standard inside widths and roller diameters. The most commonly used motorcycle pitches are $\frac{3}{8}$in, $\frac{1}{2}$in and $\frac{5}{8}$in (9.53, 12.70 and 15.88mm) but $\frac{7}{16}$in (11.12mm) has been employed also. Chain strength increases with pitch, owing to the thicker materials, but the maximum usable speed decreases because of the rise in weight; the smaller pitches are therefore selected for primary, camshaft and auxiliary drives, and the larger ones for the relatively slow rear drives.

Where a single-row roller chain has inadequate strength or bearing area for a particularly duty, and a larger pitch is impracticable, a two-row (duplex) or three-row (triplex) type can be adopted. Bearing area – which governs the wear-life – increases proportionately to the number of rows, but the breaking strength rises rather less, due to the higher bending

stresses in the longer pins.

The inverted-tooth chain, of which the Morse Hy-Vo is today's best-known example in the motor cycle field, consists only of multiple link plates and connecting pins. Each link plate has two pointed lateral projections forming teeth which engage corresponding teeth on the sprockets. Along each side of the chain are deeper plates without teeth; these plates overlap the edges of the sprockets to provide a means of location. A feature of the Hy-Vo chain is the use of side-by-side half-pins which give a rolling rather than a sliding action around the sprocket.

Again, there are various standard pitches and widths. Because of the absence of rollers, however, finer width variations are practicable than for roller chains, the minimum difference being only the thickness of two link plates. The relationships between the width and the strength and bearing area are as for the roller chain.

Makers of inverted-tooth chains maintain that their products are the more suitable for high-speed, high-power transmissions, such as primary drives from potent motor cycle engines. However, their claims for higher speeds and efficiencies, with improved smoothness, quietness and durability, are hotly contested by the roller-chain manufacturers who remain convinced that anything the inverted-tooth chain can do, the roller chain can do just as well. The issue here is still undecided, although Morse have succeeded in interesting several well known European and Japanese motor cycle companies (including Honda) in the Hy-Vo chain for primary drives.

Chain drive technology

A chain's working load is the pull due to the power being transmitted plus the centrifugal pull round the sprockets. To obviate chain breakage and ensure reasonable life, this working load must give an adequate factor of safety on the chain's breaking strength and must not overload bearings.

Let us assume that an engine has a maximum output of 30bhp at 8000rpm, and has a $\frac{3}{8}$in pitch duplex primary chain running on a 21-tooth engine sprocket.

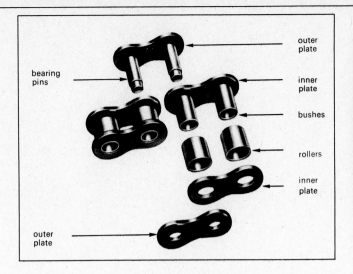

Above far left: a duplex chain in use on the rear of a drag-racing bike campaigned in Britain by John Hobbs

Above left: the Laverda 2 250TR with a totally enclosed secondary chain; the concertina section permits adjustment

Above: the components of a roller chain link

Above right: the duplex chain of the Norton Commando was kept taut by a hydraulically operated tensioner pressing a pad against each of the chain runs

Left: the secondary chain on a 250cc Bultaco Pursang

$$\text{Chain speed} = \frac{\text{teeth (21)} \times \text{pitch (0.375)} \times \text{rpm (8000)}}{12}$$
$$= 5250\text{ft per min}$$

$$\text{Load pull} = \frac{\text{hp (30)} \times 33,000}{\text{chain speed (5250)}} = \mathbf{188.6lb}$$

Centrifugal pull =
$$\frac{\text{chain wt, lb per ft} \times (\text{chain sp, ft per sec})^2}{32.2}$$
$$= \frac{0.50}{32.2} \times \left\{ \frac{5250}{60} \right\}^2 = \mathbf{118.9lb}$$

Working load = 188.6 + 118.9 = **307.5lb**
This chain (which, as just indicated, weighs 0.50lb per ft) has a breaking strength of 3900lb and a nominal bearing area of 0.034in².

$$\text{Factor of safety} = \frac{\text{breaking load}}{\text{working load}} = \frac{3900}{307.5} = \mathbf{12.7}$$

$$\text{Bearing pressure} = \frac{\text{working load}}{\text{bearing area}} = \frac{307.5}{0.034} = \mathbf{9044lb\ per\ sq\ in}$$

The factor of safety is clearly ample but the bearing pressure is high and so chain life would be short if full engine power were transmitted continuously. However, since the *average* horsepower delivered, in non-racing conditions, would probably be well under half the maximum, the chain should have a reasonable life if properly lubricated.

Since a chain comprises a series of rigidly connected hinges, a sprocket is actually a regular polygon, not a circle. The tangential speed of a rotating object varies with the radius, so the effect of the polygon is to cause the chain speed to fluctuate; the drive is therefore not inherently smooth (as it can be with a belt).

As the number of teeth is increased, the polygonal speed fluctuation falls off (rapidly at first) until by 19 teeth it is generally too small to be significant. If drive smoothness is critical, however, a relatively small-pitch wide chain is better than the equivalent longer-pitch narrower one on account of the larger number of teeth on a sprocket of given diameter. The special pin design of the Morse Hy-Vo chain compensates theoretically to some extent for the polygonal effect, because the rolling action under articulation causes the pitch to increase slightly from its nominal value.

Wear, adjustment and lubrication
A chain does not 'stretch' in service: it becomes *elongated* due to frictional wear in the joints, and the pitch therefore gets slightly greater. Until the wear is quite advanced, an inverted-tooth chain continues to engage the sprocket correctly as its pitch increases, merely riding higher up the teeth. Owing to the different geometry, a roller-chain drive tends to be less tolerant; pitch elongation gradually leads to mis-meshing of the rollers, thus accelerating the wear rate of the sprocket teeth. With either type, however, it is wise to renew a chain that has lengthened by $2\frac{1}{2}\%$.

A slack chain runs more noisily and harshly than one in correct adjustment – that is, with only a little up-and-down free movement at the middle of the run between the sprockets. Some means of adjustment or tensioning is consequently desirable on roller-chain drives, the simplest being to vary the distance between the sprockets; on motor cycle rear drives this is done by moving the wheel.

Primary chains used to be adjusted similarly by moving the gearbox, but now that unit construction is general, the best tensioning arrangement is the adjustable 'slipper' pad, bearing on the back of the chain (on the run that is normally slack) and faced with anti-wear material. Slipper adjustment is usually manual, although the Norton Commando featured an ingenious Renold-designed automatic adjuster based on an oil-pressure-actuated unit widely used for camshaft drives in car and lorry engines. Spring-loaded blade tensioners have been employed satisfactorily on motor cycle camshaft drives because the load pull, unlike that of a primary or rear chain, is not subject to drive/overrun reversals which would overcome the spring-loading.

The many bearings of a chain (particularly a heavily loaded one running at high speed) must have effective lubrication if they are not to wear prematurely, leading to noisy and less efficient running. A primary chain must therefore operate in an oilbath or, better still, be pressure-lubricated by jets. Oil-mist or splash lubrication is generally acceptable for camshaft chains, but the poor rear chain – rarely enclosed and hence bombarded with road dirt and water – has to get by on greasing during manufacture and the periodic squirt from an oil can. AB

A Machine with Many Hearts

The firm of Chater Lea was well equipped to undertake the manufacture of lugs and fittings for the makers of frames, having been in business for some ten years before the demand came for motor cycles at the turn of the century. The firm was incorporated and called the Chater Lea Manufacturing Company Limited in 1900, with Mr William Chater Lea director. The quality of their products was high and there were probably few frames running around propelled by internal combustion engines which did not incorporate some or all frame components made by this London firm in their Golden Lane works, where they remained until 1912 when the Banner Street premises were acquired.

So jealous was the firm of their reputation for producing only products of the very highest quality that it constantly advertised warnings to prospective purchasers to 'beware of imitations', to look for proof that the parts were genuine Chater Lea and if in doubt, components should be sent to the works for inspection and confirmation at no cost to the purchaser.

The Company became more ambitious and naturally developed from selling merely the components for frames to providing frames already completed. The Company made frames to fit any type of engine. Machines were produced as early as 1900 with clip-on type of engines. The ultimate step was taken in 1903 when Chater Lea produced their first complete motor cycle. Perhaps the word 'complete' is slightly misleading in a history which endeavours to be accurate,

Far left: Dougal Marchant with a 350cc Chater Lea at Brooklands in 1923

Above: Chater Lea produced their first complete machine in 1903

Left: W. D. Marchant works on his Chater Lea at Brooklands in March 1924

as the Company made the offer of the whole machine save for the tyres and saddle which the buyer was obliged to provide for himself.

At the 1908 Stanley Show, in addition to new motor cycles, Chater Lea had on display the Carette, costing 95 guineas. This machine was built with a 6hp engine (to which had been added a new type of three speed gear) fitted transversely in the frame. Also shown was a lightweight motor cycle with a 2½hp JAP engine, although the machine actually exhibited was incomplete! The sidecar outfit also used a 6hp twin-cylinder engine, with magneto ignition and chain drive via a two-speed gear box which incorporated a Chater Lea clutch. The display reflected in all their exhibits the high standard of workmanship which was the hallmark of Chater Lea.

The first Chater Lea entry in the Isle of Man TT races was in 1908, the second year these events were held. This was the private entry of C. B. Franklin who rode in the single cylinder class on his 3½hp JAP engined machine. The riders had to complete ten laps of the course, taking them over a total distance of 158 miles 220 yards, and Jack Marshall on a Triumph won the race at an average of over 40mph, and Franklin put in a fine performance to finish in sixth place. Finishing at all was an achievement as the machines were not so reliable as they are today and the road conditions were treacherous, frequently taking their toll in accidents and punctures due to the rough surfaces.

During the same year, an interesting adventure was undertaken by another private owner, W. B. Gibb, who, with his wife in the sidecar, toured Scotland on a Chater Lea 'Dreadnought' in a fortnight, covering a thousand miles. The machine was fitted with a 5hp Peugeot engine, with a three-speed gearbox. At a time when machine reliability was a luxury, the only troubles encountered by Mr. Gibb on his lengthy tour were pulled out belt fasteners and a solitary puncture. This achievement spoke volumes not only for the pluck of the rider, but also for the confidence he had in his Chater Lea, and the latter lived up to its reputation. History does not record the sentiments of Mrs Gibb after she climbed out of the Mills Fulford Wicker side car after a thousand miles of Scottish highways and byways, but perhaps this is just as well.

Over a dozen different makes of engine were fitted to Chater Lea motor cycles and had the Guinness book of records been publishing in the early days of the century no doubt the entry for the record number of different engine makes, sizes and dimensions for one motor cycle manufacturer would have named Chater Lea. The variety included British and foreign engines, singles and twins, but up to the war years, the Company showed a distinct preference for big twin-cylinder machines, mainly for use with sidecars. Spring frames were tried but like all predecessors from other factories, these were unsuccessful with the result that good rigid frames were

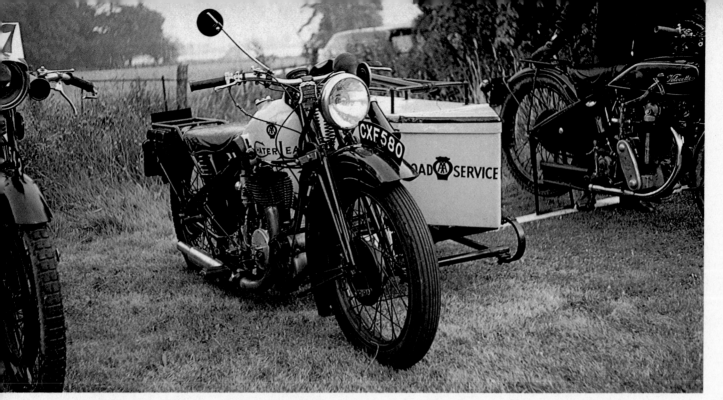

favoured. Chater Lea technology showed itself, however, in the patterns of front forks, which were, if anything, ahead of their time. On the only other pre-war Chater Lea entry in the 1910 TT single cylinder class unfortunately N. E. Drury was not ahead of his, or any other persons' time, being obliged to retire. For 1912, Chater Lea continued the model 7, three-speed chain drive sidecar machine.

During World War I, production of motor cycles ceased and the Company concentrated on production of small shells, wire cutters, terminals and other items for military purposes.

Motor cycle production recommenced in 1919 with the big twin machines being the main offerings, although the lightweight 2¼ was also available. It was in this year that A.C. Woodman joined the company and was responsible for the design of all engines produced by the firm. By 1922 the swing to single cylinder engined machines encouraged the adoption of the Blackburne 350cc overhead valve engine for solo machines and the 545cc side valve engine mainly used for sidecar outfits. By the middle of the decade Chater Lea were to incorporate a single cylinder 350cc engine of their own manufacture, fitted to their sporting model. W. D. Marchant developed the engine for racing and achieved considerable success at the Brookland's track. Marchant was employed by Burney and Blackburne Limited, as tuner and development engineer and he chose the Chater Lea frame as he considered it the best for the purpose. Dougal Marchant was responsible for the success both in the workshop and on the track, tuning and racing the machines. In 1923 alone, eleven world records were achieved at Brooklands, together with a win in both

the 100 mile and 200 mile sidecar class for 350cc machines. Marchant was ably supported by another successful rider, R. H. Hopkins.

The 350cc OHV and the 545cc side valve models were introduced to the public at the 1922 Show and the Company highlighted the features of interchangeable wheels and all-chain drive. Other models included the renowned big twin and a small two-stroke. Prices for motor cycles were not cheap even back in the twenties and the 350cc OHV was priced at £72 and even the two-stroke lightweight with a Villiers 269cc engine retailed at £42.10.0 (£42.50).

The Blackburne 348cc pushrod OHV and the 545 side-valve engines fitted to the Chater Lea, were compact and well made, and notable for the interchangeability of parts. The outside flywheel of these engines made them readily identifiable, and the excellence of performance endeared them to their owners, the 350cc OHV as a sports mount and the 545cc as a sound 'slogger', ideal for sidecar work.

Racing success at Brooklands no doubt influenced sales and by 1924 saddle tanks were fitted to the Blackburne engined models. A trend towards the motor cycle for commercial use was evident and Chater Lea was well able to provide sturdy outfits capable of undertaking delivery of goods or other similar tasks at an economical cost. Their renowned quality stood them in good stead and they were able to withstand rough handling as might be expected when in commercial use. Amongst the purchasers of Chater Lea motor cycles were the Automobile Association who, from the early twenties, provided their patrol men firstly with the Villiers engined model

Above: the AA used Chater Lea combinations from the early 1920s until 1936. This is the 545cc Blackburne engined machine, which was ideal for sidecars work

Below: the Chater Lea of 1926 was fitted with a 350cc ohv Blackburne engine and was a fine sports-touring machine

fitted with a small box carrier, and thereafter with the 545cc model. The Automobile Association continued to use Chater Lea motor cycles in the 1930s and were the last customers of the Company as far as motor cycles were concerned, placing their last order in 1936.

Marchant's overhead camshaft engine made a spectacular debut in March 1925, achieving 100mph and making it the world's fastest 350cc machine. Subsequent record attacks resulted in nineteen British and World records being secured, proving reliability as well as speed, for the records ranged in distance from one kilometre to 200 miles. The machine upon which Marchant achieved these successes was an OHC adapted by him from a Blackburne push-rod engine and was of the vertical shaft type, with the camshaft driven by bevel gears. The compression ratio used was 7:1 and the fuel used was alcohol. The light construction of the machine undoubtedly contributed to its speed.

The success of Marchant's OHC engine had inspired Woodman to design the famous 'face cam' engine which was introduced to the public at the 1925 show.

The specification of the Woodman 348cc OHC machine included a Binks carburettor, ML magneto, all chain drive and the not inconsiderable price ticket of £80. It might not have been cheap, but it was definitely good value

for money. The 1925 Show exhibits were almost entirely made up of the Company's sporting machines. The 'overhead camshaft' engine was offered to the public for the coming year. The inverted commas are used because the method of operating the rockers was by 'face cam' unlike other types such as the Velocette designed two years earlier, which used a bevel drive to the camshaft, the cams directly operating the valves via the rockers. The 1925 'face cam' engine was designed for high speed and reliability, incorporating an unusual method of valve operation, two face cams being fitted to the top of the hollow vertical shaft, splined at both ends and driven by a bevel from the main shaft. The cam 'plates' were mounted one above the other at the top of the shaft with the inlet uppermost, so that the rockers followed the contours on the cams. The vertical shaft became, in effect, the camshaft, so it could not be accurately described as an OHC. The whole was contained in a solid rocker box casting, using an aluminium washer on the cylinder head, resulting in an oil-tight engine, an unusual feature at that time. The magneto was driven from the off side mainshaft and to ensure good lubrication two oil pumps were used; one supplying the rocker box, oil running by gravity to a spiral pump at the base of the camshaft, then up the hollow shaft to the valve actuating mechanism; the surplus oil returned to the oil tank through a sight feed. The second was via Best and Lloyd pump which fed directly into the crankcase, without a return to the oil tank, as

lubrication of the bottom half of the engine was by splash. A 6 to 1 compression ratio was used for touring, but higher ratio pistons could be fitted for racing on alcohol fuels. The design was considered excellent, as was the workmanship on the finished product, undoubtedly Chater Lea's finest achievement. To convey the principal, one eminent journalist likened the valve operation to that of a tone arm running on a warped gramophone record!

From 1930 the motor cycle production side of the Company was gradually run down although machines were still available and indeed the Company exhibited at the 1931, 1933 and 1934 shows. In 1930 the Company continued to offer the 348cc OHC, the side valve 545cc and the two-stroke Villers models' and machines were available until 1936 when motor cycle production at Chater Lea ceased.

The company changed its name to Chater Lea Limited and, at the death of William Chater Lea, in 1927 the founder of the company and his two sons, John and Bernard, decided to move the works to Letchworth the following year, forming another company Chater Lea Estates Limited to control the Banner Street property, and revert to Chater Lea Manufacturing Limited for the business. The Banner Street works were subsequently severely damaged by enemy action during World War II. The company continued in operation and flourishes today after some 86 years of trading, still with a Chater Lea at the helm. Indeed, an enviable record.   ET

the framework of motocross

When it comes to motocross engineering, it would not be an exaggeration to say that Eric Cheney borders on genius: if he cannot cure a problem, it is incurable; if he says it will not work, then it will not work. That at least comes from inside the head of someone who is mechanically minded to an extraordinary degree, and from a wealth of experience earned the hard way – as a bread-and-butter motocross rider. His story goes back thirty years when he was only nineteen but had already seen some gruesome sights. The war and its ravages had not escaped him due to the Royal Navy finding him a job watching the Russian convoys.

Having survived those cold and miserable days, he began enjoying the more pleasant surroundings of Parkstone in Dorset where he became a

mechanic for the local Triumph agents. It was the thirst for competition that he wanted to quench, however; so, with an ex-WD Triumph single, he launched himself into the world of motocross. It was hardly a bike fit for a champion but nevertheless he showed style and promise. 'The next bike I got was an Ariel Red Hunter which had been damaged in an accident. I put it into scrambles trim and ran that for a while until I got a real scrambles bike. It was another Ariel, a 500, which at the time was thought to be very modern. You will laugh I suppose but it had telescopic forks and a swinging arm,' he said. Cheney, gaining in confidence and ability, entered some of the more important events in the south of England. One of those was the Sunbeam Point-to-Point where he took the 500cc class cup.

It was during this successful period that Cheney became noticed, first by Ariels who signed him up as a works rider and later by the ACU who chose him to ride in the British team in the Moto Cross des Nations held that year in Sweden. He was also a team member the next year when the event was staged in Belgium. Eric was now an established motocross rider and he felt, quite rightly, that he could earn a living doing what he liked doing most so he went to France with another top rider of the day, Les Archer; these two on Nortons had many successes. Then, in 1957, Cheney swopped bikes again. This time it was the ex-Bill Nilsson BSA which took his fancy and, in company with Phil Nex also on a BSA, he went on the continental circus once more. He remembers this year as being the best one he ever had with fifteen wins and six seconds to his credit.

He continued into the late 1950s and unsuccessfully tried to change to a

Below: Eric Cheney, pictured in 1967, astride a Cheney-Victor outside his back garden workshop in Fleet, Hampshire with two of his staff

Triumph twin; it was no good, for he had spent too many hours in the saddle of a big single to learn a new technique. So, for 1960 he was back to his old love – but not for long. Whilst competing in Algiers he became ill. 'I picked up some sort of a germ in the blood and it put me right out of the game: I was useless for a long time after that. Probably I tried to get back into it too soon but I realised that scrambling was over for me,' he explains. The year was 1961 but that is not the end of the story but only the end of the first book. As Eric's riding career was coming to a close, he made himself yet another special. He took a 497cc AJS, some Norton forks and wheels and attached them to a frame of his own design and here he discovered his forte – machine preparation.

Now denied the pleasure of riding, he could not stay away from meetings. Motocross was in his blood and nothing could kill it, not even an

Algierian bug. Cheney decided that if he could not ride the bikes he would settle then for those who could, those like the late Jerry Scott. 'One weekend I went to an event at Beenham Park in Berkshire and was watching this lad going round and thought he had the right idea but his bike was letting him down. Anyway, I had a chat to him and asked him if he would like to bring it over to my place and see if we could not sort it out.' He did sort it out because Jerry Scott on the Cheney Gold Star became a nationwide winner and won good publicity for Eric during the winter in the BBC *Grandstand* meetings on television. One of the important features of this machine was its low weight. 'I got the Gold Star down to 295lb, ready to race, which is not bad when you think the lowest the factory ever got their works bikes down to was about 350lb plus – which is a lot of weight to throw around.'

What makes a good engineer a great one? Nine out of ten people will tell you it is attention to detail, and a perfect example of this is Eric Cheney. Look at any motor cycle which he has put together and you will see the

meticulous way he finishes the job – neat and tidy down to the last nut and bolt, with welds executed with beautiful precision. It is hardly surprising that some of the most discerning motor cyclists the world over come to Hampshire to have their engines mounted in a Cheney frame. Could it be the attraction of having something designed solely for you because, with Cheney, every order starts from square one. 'I take every frame I make from ground level. Someone will bring me the engine and tell me what he wants and we work things out from there. You get the head angle right then you look at the trail which is very important. Suspension is also vital especially these days with the power some of these bikes are turning out, and from there we turn to the main components of the frame.'

During his many years as a frame builder, Eric has wrapped a large variety of engines into his well tailored tubes. After the first one in 1962 to take the big 500 AJS, he turned to the BSA Gold Star, a combination which was very successful for him. With Small Heath turning to a smaller unit,

Below: Cheney accepts orders from all over the world to build motocross machines using his frames. Pictured is a Cheney-Yamaha, a 1969 250cc bike

Cheney was asked by many riders to do what he did for the Gold Star. So, along came the Cheney Victor on the motocross scene. With the ISDT Selectors trying desperately to keep the team on British machines, they brought their 650cc Triumphs to Cheyney's Fleet, Hampshire, factory to have frames made for them. Here again, Eric has first-hand experience of what the ISDT is all about. In 1950, he entered this gruelling event on a 500cc Triumph and won a gold medal. Large or small, four-stroke or two-stroke, he will make a custom built frame for any motor cycle. 'I have made them for the big Suzukis and for the little 125cc Sachs from Austria. I have made them for Honda XLs, the 250 and 350 and also the 450. I had a order from a man in Sweden to make a frame for Husqvarnas; we got 25 made, then they took exception to it and cut off his supply of engines. The arrangement I had with Vic Camp for the Ducati was like that, too. We started off well then the supply of engines dried up.' As one door closes another opens, however, and in 1977 a friend of Eric in France was keeping him busy: he ordered 75 frames in the last three months of 1976.

Perhaps the most ambitious frame yet made by the Hampshire engineer was the monoshock model. By doing away with the two rear suspension-units and attaching the swinging arm to one large shock absorber running longitudinally under the tank, rear suspension was revolutionised. 'I think this is where the answer lies for the future. I tried a double unit which was fine for an enduro bike but, on a tough motocross circuit, it overheated. I tried putting the shock absorber inside the top tube and attaching it to the steering head to give you a longer strut and less oscillation but again had this overheating problem. Mind you, I think that with technology improving, the quality of the units the idea of the monoshock will become a real possibility in the future.' Who better to predict what engineers will do for motocross in the years to come than a man who himself has spent many years in the game: Eric Cheney.   RB

Right: five times British 500cc motocross champion, John Banks rode Cheney bikes throughout 1973 but the BSA engine was not considered sufficiently competitive to enter the machines for the World Championship

MOPEDS and MINI-BIKES

The motor cycle industry of Italy has always produced a vast number of 50cc lightweight motor cycles and mopeds, and they are still being produced in abundance, in every possible shape and size imaginable. One of the leading makers in this category of machine is Cimatti, the company's name being Cimatti Enrico SpA. It is a family business, the managing director being Enrico, a young engineer, and son of the founder Marco. Although 50cc motor cycles are the mainstay of production, larger models have been made in the past, which dates back until just a short time before World War II.

Marco Cimatti was, in fact, a cycle fanatic, and a very successful racer. In 1932, he won a gold medal in the Olympic Games in the Italian cycle team, and naturally became a very well known sportsman. Being so involved with bicycles, and with a good reputation, too, he decided to go into bicycle production. So, the first small Cimatti factory was born in 1937, at a small town called Porta Lame; business was good, but sadly the factory was completely destroyed during the war years.

However, this was no insurmountable problem to the ever enthusiastic Marco Cimatti: in 1946, he restarted bicycle production and, in 1950, branched out into motor cycle production. This was in an era when motor cycles of every type found buyers, and the almost insatiable demand enabled him to build up his equipment and techniques to a high and modern standard. While rival manufacturers producing larger and more expensive machines fell by the wayside in later years through the worldwide sales slump, Marco Cimatti was able to carry on regardless, and today the position of the factory is high in the Italian motor cycle league table. The factory was relocated in 1960 at Pioppe di Salvaro, in the Appenines, where it remains in the 1970s. There has not been a great deal of Cimatti activity in motor cycle sport, the factory preferring to concentrate on producing the machines for the 'man in the street', where the potential is greater. Nevertheless, there have been a few sporting efforts, the most notable being those in 1966–7–8, when Cimatti machines won the 50cc Italian trials championships outright.

The 50cc motor cycles made by Cimatti today cover a wide range, to suit everyone from the district nurse to the youngster making for the nearest coffee emporium in the shortest possible time! In fact, this type of range has been covered by the company for some years now, although a steady programme of research and development is adhered to.

In the past, however, some larger and even more varied models were in the line-up. In 1965, for instance, the 50cc line included a rather neat motor scooter, the complete rear enclosure folding forwards to reveal the engine unit and the fully enclosed transmission; at the same time, a variety of those typical Italian three-wheeler trucks were produced.

After the sporting successes in trials in the mid 1960s, later years saw three very attractive Cimatti motor cycles in production: the 100cc and 175cc Sport Lusso models were for the road while, for motocross, the Kaiman Cross Competizione was produced. All used four-speed gearboxes, and the 'Cross' was claimed to produce 19.5bhp at 7000rpm. Strangely enough, the models did not stay in production for long. They were

Below: following successes in trials during the mid 1960s Cimatti produced the Kaiman Trial for off-road motor cycling. A 50cc machine reputed to produce 12bhp at 7000rpm, the Kaiman is available with four or six-speed transmission

Below: Cimatti's 50cc moped-style '86' has four gears, alloy wheels, and the U-shaped frame forms the petrol tank

Bottom: the company produces a range of mini-bikes, popular with younger riders, and this is the 'Bobcat', fitted with a 50cc Morini Franco engine and four-speed transmission

very well designed and built, and performed well, but Cimatti preferred, it seemed, to stick tight to the 50cc class where he had made his name.

1972 saw a couple of new 125cc models in the line, one for motocross, with a five-speed gearbox, and the other for the road. Named the Airete 5/M, its Morini two-stroke engine produced 15bhp on a compression of 9 to 1. Detail changes were made afterwards, but for 1977 it was also missing from the line-up.

Cimatti, in fact, have never entered the business of engine manufacture: always proprietry engines have been utilised, mostly Minarellis or those of Moto Morini, and all two-stroke type.

Under the direction of Enrico Cimatti, the company has adopted a policy of pushing hard for export sales, and this has been achieved. The machines have proved popular in the lucrative US market, and in many others including France, Norway and even Tunisia! Production is in the region of 50,000 units per year, while the number of employees number around a hundred – a fair guide to the standard of automation achieved at the Cimatti plant.

While a new 125cc enduro style Cimatti is under development, the 1977 range is made up solely of 50cc machines. The Chic is the only true sedate moped, and has one gear with automatic clutch, but can be supplied with footrests to order. More stylish is the model 86 with a U-tube frame holding the fuel, four gears and alloy wheels. Mini bikes form a large part of Cimatti production, too. The Mini-Chic and automatic model start the line, while ten inch diameter alloy wheels and an upswept exhaust system feature on the sturdy little Bob Cat, the next step up. The Bat Boy and Bat Baby are most definitely for juniors, as is the Mini Prix which is a new introduction.

The Kaiman Trial is available with either four or six-speed engine/gearbox units, and has a strong duplex frame; it is a fun machine for on or off the road. Finally, there is the Sagittario, fitted with pedals and footrests for licensing reasons with a six-speed gearbox fitted as standard. It is very stylish and features dropped handlebars and a long narrow fuel tank blended into the seat; the whole sits astride a strong duplex frame. Naturally, it appeals very much to the younger rider who has a few years to go before he is able, or allowed, to ride a 250 or 500cc machine.

So, Cimatti in 1977 are as healthy as ever even though they stick to the 'standard Italian' 50cc do-everything machine. It could be that they will continue to prosper as long as every Italian realises that, aside from walking, 'small biking' is the cheapest way to go DJ

Lightweights and Fours from Ohio

It is an odd but inescapable fact that, in spite of the former greatness of her native motor cycle industry, the USA has only once produced a truly successful two-stroke lightweight. It is not for the want of trying, either. Around 1916, Indian made an attempt with a pretty little two-fifty and a year later, Excelsior (in other words, the Schwinn Bicycle Company, of Chicago) followed up with a 269cc two-stroke bike which was most probably a Triumph Junior made under licence. Both projects were very short-lived, however, and had gone within a season or so.

The sole exception was the little Cleveland, built in the Ohio city of that name by the Cleveland Motorcycle Manufacturing Company between 1915 and 1927. Here, too, a certain degree of Triumph influence could be detected: early examples featured a cylindrical fuel tank slung from the frame top rail by two metal straps, as on the

Triumph, while even more noticeable was the front fork, pivoted at the base of the steering head and operating in a fore-and-aft plane under the control of a horizontal coil spring. Why, the first Cleveland (introduced in July of 1915) even had a Brown and Barlow carburettor and a genuine, English-made Brooks leather-topped saddle! There, however, the resemblance ended. The engine was a conventional 222cc single (63.5mm × 69.8mm bore and stroke) but turned around so that the crankshaft was in line with the frame; this was coupled directly to a two-speed gearbox, which meant that a worm mechanism was necessary, in order to provide for chain final drive.

Overall gear ratios were 5 to 1, and 10 to 1 and, unusually, the gearbox and rear wheel sprockets were of the same diameter. A striking feature of this model, and of Clevelands for many years to come, was a frame in which the power

unit was carried by a duplex tubular structure, the straight tubes passing each side of the engine at about crankcase-mouth height. Its claimed performance was 35mph and 120mpg.

During the years of World War I, Cleveland sales were restricted to the USA itself but, with the return of peace came a complete redesign of the bike, coupled with a strong drive for export sales. Named the Cleveland 20, the new model was launched in the autumn of 1919. The design of the engine-gear unit

278

looked much as before, except that capacity had gone up to 269cc (69.85mm × 69.85mm bore and stroke); it was still a two-speeder and although the bottom-gear ratio remained at 10 to 1, the top gear had been lowered to 6 to 1. Also, the specification had gone all-American, with the adoption of a Schebler carburettor and Berling magneto as standard equipment

Much less flimsy looking than before, the frame had been strengthened by the addition of an extra rail beneath the tank – and the tank, too, was a substantial two-gallon affair, a conventional rectangular design formed from two edge-welded pressings, instead of a cylinder. The Triumph-style front fork now had pressed-steel blades, in place of the original tubular components, but in other respects it stayed as it

was and good it was, too.

The export drive began to pay off and, in an advertisement in the British motorcycle press of the day, the makers were able to claim that 'From the idea on which the construction depends, to the final enamel finish, the Cleveland stands for intelligence and skill. The product of a large and magnificently equipped plant in which money buys quality first, and quantity next, the Cleveland has made its way around the world, and been accepted as the most dependable machine in its class'.

Pinch of salt, anyone? Certainly the little machine sold reasonably well in countries such as Holland and France, but very few reached English roads, because it was at a financial disadvantage when compared with the local product. British concessionaires were North Western Motors Ltd, of Norton Street, Liverpool, and the best they could quote was £85, ex docks, with a delivery charge to be added to that – as against £65 for the popular Triumph Junior, or £70 for the corresponding 220cc Velocette two-stroke.

To the basic model was added, in 1923, the Model E Sporting Solo, fully equipped with dynamo and battery electric lighting. Ingeniously, the Splitdorf dynamo was clamped to the nearside frame cradle rail, where it was chain-driven from a sprocket on a shaft extension protruding through the rear of the gearbox.

However, the next expansion of the range was rather more of a surprise. It was the Model F25, with a similar frame and Triumph-type front fork as the two-stroke, but with a 350cc side-valve engine-gear unit, again disposed with the crankshaft in line with the frame. Like the familiar two-stroke bike, it was a two-speeder. Silchrome exhaust and chrome-nickel inlet valves were specified, and lubrication was total loss, the mechanical oil pump being supplemented by a hand unit. Two versions were catalogued, respectively with Bosch magneto ignition (at £42 10s, on the British market), or with Splitdorf dynamo and Wico coil ignition (at £49 10s).

Obviously, Cleveland were becoming four-stroke minded; indeed, they were casting envious eyes on the substantial sales being achieved by the four-in-line Henderson and Ace. The time was ripe, they felt, for Cleveland to move into the four-cylinder class – and with a sound and long established network of dealers from which to launch such a machine, it should be away to a flying start. Fortuitously, or so it seemed, one L. E. Fowler (who had learned his trade in the

This French lady and her little girl are mounted on a 1920 Cleveland 20 two-stroke, which has Triumph type front forks which move backwards and forwards rather than up and down. The lady's progress would be impeded, however, her skirt preventing the use of the long hand lever of the two-speed gearbox

Detroit car industry) now came upon the scene with a design he had just completed, and this the Cleveland management took up.

News of the newcomer broke in mid September 1925, and the factory promised that deliveries would begin on 1 October. Of only 600cc, the new bike was a T-head side-valve, with the inlet camshaft on the left, and the exhaust camshaft on the right. Cylinders were individual (and, said the works, interchangeable), and the light cast-iron pistons were carried on duralumin connecting rods the length of which was 2½ times the stroke.

The frame was of traditional Cleveland design, with the engine slung at crankcase-mouth height from two horizontal tubes but, in addition, there were torque tubes at each side, from the three-speed gearbox to the rear spindle. Other details included a single-plate clutch and Timken roller bearings in the wheel hubs. The front fork at last departed from Triumph design, and was a leading-link type similar to that of the Reading Standard, Ace or Harley-Davidson. Price, with full electric lighting, was to be £89 in Britain.

Sad to say, the 600cc Cleveland Four was a disaster. Performance was way below what had been expected, handling was only so-so and it stood no chance at all against the more established fours from other factories. Only a couple of hundred were made before production was stopped.

However, Cleveland had not given up hope, and in 1926 came news that they had signed up Everitt DeLong, a motor cycle designer who had worked for both Henderson and Ace. Very different in concept to the previous year's model, the DeLong-designed four was a 750cc, with the air-cooled cylinders in a monobloc casting. A separate monobloc casting, the cylinder head embodied the inlet manifold; valve arrangement was inlet-over-exhaust. The three-speed gearbox was bolted to the rear of the crankcase, but had the very clever feature of an end cover, on the left, through which the entire gear cluster could be extracted without first having to remove the power unit from the frame. The traditional Cleveland frame was discarded, and now the engine sat in a widely splayed, duplex cradle frame.

DeLong's machine was a comparative winner: it performed well (within its limitations) and was trouble free in operation. The truth was, however, that it was still only a 750, whereas the competition, in the form of the Henderson, had a 1301cc power unit. To help compensate for the performance differential, a sports model Cleveland was announced later in 1926, with a claimed top speed of 75 mph plus, obtained by the use of a humpier inlet camshaft, bigger valves and polished ports.

That, however, was just an interim measure and, in the meantime, DeLong was at work on a 1000cc model, the '4-61' (four cylinders, 61 cubic inches). Unveiled in 1927, this was, according to the manufacturer's advertising, 'A motorcycle that surpasses all known precedent'. Other claims were 'Quicker access to high speed than you have ever known', and 'Greater vitality and alertness'.

The drum banging could be justified, too, for at last the Cleveland company were able to offer a machine capable of taking on the opposition: the '4-61' could top 90mph. Unusually for an American-built bike, it had a front brake drum, in addition to a rear brake; a further pioneering feature was a substantial prop-stand. The engine was inlet-over-exhaust, as before, and a smooth ride was guaranteed by carrying the power unit on three-point rubber mountings from the frame cradle.

Sales began to soar, and now it seemed that the Cleveland management had the bit between their teeth, because yet another version of the four appeared at the 1929 New York Show. This was the Cleveland Tornado Four with, so it was said, a 100mph potential. The most noticeable feature of these machines was a completely new frame, in which the top tubes ran in almost a straight line from the steering head to rear spindle; in conjunction with a wedge-shaped tank, this afforded a seating position 2.5in lower than before. Pistons of the newcomer were in Dow metal, a special alloy, lighter than aluminium but of equivalent strength. The compression ratio had been raised, and inlet valves and ports increased in size. Now, too, customers had a choice of colour schemes, in the Potomac Blue of previous Cleveland models, or a bold Mephisto Red, each offset with ample gold lining to enhance looks.

Even as production of the Tornado got under way, the Cleveland drawing office was at work on something even more exciting. This was the Century, still of 1000cc, but with a further developed version of the Tornado engine; again, compression ratio had gone up, and more attention had been paid to gas-flowing the inlet ports. The frame was as before, but there was a new and heavier front fork, with triple suspension springs to strengthen things.

Most intriguing feature of all was that each Cleveland Century would have to reach 100mph on road test, a small inscribed brass plate certifying this fact being then attached to the inlet-tappet cover plate. The plate, by the way, was not added on the assembly line, but in the despatch department, after the road-tester had returned with his report.

Ultimate in Cleveland fours, the Century was to have been the 1930 season offering, but production was brought to a premature halt after only a small batch had been built. The reason, of course, was the Wall Street crash. American enthusiasts no longer had the cash to buy exotic fours, and Cleveland had no option but to close down.   FG

Below: a 1919 single-cylinder Cleveland of 269cc, which features a Schebler carburettor and a Berling magneto. This machine is now part of the impressive Harrah collection

Covering Up

The average rider comes in many varying shapes and sizes, and rides bikes of every conceivable description in all kinds of weather. Some are rich, many are poor, some regard motor cycles as a way of life, while others as an economic necessity. Some riders are fashion conscious, and for others, keeping warm and dry is the main criterion. For some, safety is paramount, for others perhaps convenience. With such a multiplicity of clothing products to choose from, where does one start.

In the pioneering days of two wheeled travel, clothing was not such a problem – merely an adaptation of what one would wear on a horse, with possibly a pair of rudimentary goggles and a flat hat to keep the wind off as one hurtled along at 15mph. However, as bikes became more sophisticated and a great deal faster, the motor cyclist became increasingly demanding. In racing, where protection and speed were essential, flapping great coats were not only cumbersome but dangerous and restrictive. So, the first leather suits made their appearance on the race track, together with modified flying helmets and goggles to protect the head and eyes; boots were reinforced with

metal toecaps and studs for efficient braking! Thus, we have the beginnings of the traditional motor cyclist's outfit.

It is perhaps a fitting tribute to those early pioneers that, even in this age of modern technology, when clothing can be devised to protect men on a surface as arid and hostile as the moon, or as cold and dangerous as the North Sea, the leather suit remains the basic means of protection for the majority of serious motor cyclists. Perhaps it is because unlike other materials, leather is a 'living' thing which requires treating with respect and which must be fed with special oils if it is to remain supple.

It is virtually impossible to design the

ideal suit, for it would have to fulfill so many varying functions. Warm in winter, it has to be light, yet waterproof. Capable of being kept clean, yet available in bright colours for safety. Easy to get into, yet tight fitting for streamlining and comfort. Durable yet not prohibitively expensive. Whereas the driver of any modern car has a controlled environment and can adjust his heating and ventilation system to suit conditions, the motor cyclist is at the mercy of the elements. It is an ironic state of affairs that the engine of a motor cycle produces so

Above: wet-weather riding is made more tolerable by a waterproof suit such as this one

Left: adequate boots are an essential rather than a luxury

much excess heat that designers go to extraordinary lengths to dissipate it through adding fins, black paint or even electric fans and radiators. Yet, despite this, on a cold day it is possible to turn numb in even the best clothing. Conversely, in the height of summer, because it is essential to wear protective clothing for safety sake, riding in town can be unbearingly stifling.

Safety is often the last factor when choosing the right type of clothing, yet there is no knowing when, without warning, it may become the most important. Some riders will quite happily fork out thousands of pounds on a motor cycle, yet when it comes to buying a sensible helmet and some gloves, they will often be reluctant to part with a penny more than they have to. One example is in the colour of suits. This is in spite of official government research which shows that 70% of accidents involving motor cycles occur because car drivers were unable to see the rider; black, however, remains the cheapest and the most popular colour. Many younger riders will happily trip around in ordinary clothes struggling to change gear in platform shoes. Just how much protection a tee shirt will afford in the event of a

twenty yard slide along a tarmaced road, can only be left to the imagination.

By and large, motor cycle clothing is cheap in comparison to the actual cost of a motor cycle, consequently a massive industry has developed to supply the market with a bewildering range of clothing.

Suits

A suit or jacket is usually the first item of clothing to be purchased after the legally necessary helmet. Ninety per cent of suits are made from four basic materials, leather, wax cotton, pvc and nylon, and are available as one or two piece outfits, lined or unlined. Leather is the traditional material for clothing the motor cyclist, and the most expensive.

Jackets begin at around £35 but can be double that for the better designs; trousers range from £30 to £60 and complete suits from around £60 to £150. The majority of suits are available in standard sizes, but can usually be made to measure, with a specialist firm charging around £20 for this service. With this amount of money at stake, it is essential to consult a reputable firm for advice, for often only an expert can tell the difference between a poor and a good quality hide.

Suits come in two designs, racing or touring. The former are designed to fit the rider snugly when in a crouched position, whereas a touring suit has a looser cut, designed to be worn in the upright position, and often has pockets.

Regular maintenance is essential to ensure suits remain in good condition. When wet, they should never be dried in direct heat, and cleaning should be done with saddle soap, after which a dressing of Connolly's Hide Food, or Neatsfoot oil should be applied.

Unfortunately, leather, although windproof and warm, is not particularly waterproof, hence an oversuit is essential for wet weather riding. For many years, this has meant a suit made of waxed cotton, *ie*, material impregnated with wax. When new, waxed cotton is completely waterproof in the most arduous conditions. However, without reproofing, it can sometimes become pervious after several years use. The main drawback of waxed cotton suits is that the wax tends

Above right, left to right: a waterproof jacket of heavy nylon with wrap-over front; waterproof over-trousers; a selection of gauntlets and a balaclava

Left: traditional protection is the leather suit; this is a two-piece type

Below: a legal requirement as well as an obvious protection is a crash helmet. A wide variety of open and full face types are available to suit personal tastes

to attract road dirt, and consequently suits are liable to become extremely grubby and unsuitable for wearing indoors.

Any attempt at cleaning could lessen its waterproof qualities and eventually the whole suit may have to be sent away for cleaning and reproofing – an expensive and time consuming process. They are not particularly cheap either, some makes retailing at around £40 to £50.

Poly vinyl carbonate is not in itself a new material, and its waterproof qualities would suggest it as ideal for motor cyclists. Yet, it never really caught the imagination of riders, possibly because it is not a very flattering material and, in cold weather, can get fairly brittle, which leads to damage.

The recent appearance of nylon suits in the shops has to a degree coincided with the sudden upsurge in popularity of the motor cycle. For many newcomers on two wheels, it represents a sensible first suit. The most widely used material is 'Dunloprufe' nylon, a combination of nylon and polyurethane. One newcomer to the field is 'Brollybond' nylon, a material developed in America which consists of a layer of very thin supple plastic sandwiched in between two layers of nylon.

'Dunloprufe' is itself completely waterproof, but the problem is always with the seams which have to be doped. Sometimes, the process is unsuccessful, or perhaps a jacket is too small, causing the seams to stretch and water to seep in. A wide range of styles are available in nylon with bright colours as an added safety factor. There are other advantages: a nylon suit can be kept relatively clean, and when wet will dry very quickly. It can be folded into a relatively small space for storage, will not crumple, and can be used with a wide range of modern fastenings including velcro, and nylon zips. A basic one piece unlined suit can be obtained for as little as £12, although a de luxe, quilt lined two piece could cost up to £45.

Head protection

Helmets are required by law for both the rider and the passenger, and must conform to specific standards set by the British Standards Institute. There are two main designs, full face helmets, sometimes called integral models, and open or jet style helmets. Within these two categories, there is once again a large selection to choose from. Generally speaking, the more money you pay, the better the helmet. Obviously, the owner of a moped does not necessarily need the same level of protection as a road racer, but the serious rider should, by and large, buy the best new helmet he can afford. Two materials are available, glassfibre and plycarbonate. To the extent that polycarbonate helmets can be mass-produced, they are usually cheaper, although vulnerable to various solvents and cannot be painted.

Integral helmets have only been widely available for about ten years now, yet the added facial protection afforded by the front chin protector, and the extra comfort of the wrap around visor has made them a popular choice for many. Visors themselves come in many different forms, clear or tinted, flexible or rigid, with air holes or even heating elements! In addition, flimsy plastic rip offs can be used to protect a visor from scratching. Goggles can only be used successfully with open helmets and are gradually going out of fashion as virtually all helmets now come complete with a visor.

In winter, many motor cyclists choose to wear a balaclava to eliminate draughts and prevent long hair from interfering with vision. Here, the most expensive are the silk variety at around £4, although cheaper versions are available in cotton or rayon.

The really dedicated motor cyclist can even obtain helmet pelmets which stick to the front of an integral helmet with velcro tape and protect the throat.

Gloves

At times, particularly in summer, gloves may seem like an expensive luxury, but it is only when you stop to consider how most people react in an accident

Below right: special protection for loose surface competition includes visor, goggles and 'muzzle' to protect from flying stones

Below: for rough riding, supple plastic leg and shoulder guards are useful protection

(they instinctively put out their hands to break a fall) that their worth is realised. Hence, a good pair of leather gloves are essential. Both conventional fingered styles and gauntlets are readily available and come with or without a variety of linings – sheepskin, nylon and nylon/foam being the most common. In summer, thin racing type gloves are often adequate, although in winter, it is sometimes advisable to wear thin gloves underneath, made from artificial silk. In wet weather, nylon or waxed cotton overmitts will prevent leather gloves from becoming damp. Gloves range in price from around £5 to £15, silk inners are about £1, and overmitts £3 to £4. If, after all this, your hands are still cold, then as a last resort, it's possible to fit handlebar muffs. These are plastic covers that slip over the handlebar grips and provide protection for the hands. They obviously take some time to get used to, but can be a real boon in wet weather.

Boots

Leather motor cycle boots range in price from £15 for the simplest unlined version, to around £60 for exotic moto-cross boots. It is a fallacy to imagine that ordinary boots will suffice for motor cycling: proper boots have specially strengthened heels to take the extra knocks when riding, steel reinforcement at strategic points and leather reinforcements where the foot is used to change gear. Leather boots, like suits, are not waterproof, although regular treatment with dubbin wax can help. For bad weather riding, nylon spats or rubber overboots are available.

Miscellaneous

Always quick to develop a market,

numerous other items have been devised by manufacturers to tempt the unwary. Take, for example, body belts. Used primarily by sports riders on rough ground, it is claimed they reduce travel sickness, and that queasy feeling when riding over uneven surfaces. Silk scarves can often look attractive especially if obtained with the motor cycle manufacturers logo. Reflective and fluorescent over jackets, they are a useful way of remaining conspicuous at night, although it must be remembered that orange or green fluorescent jackets only seem bright in daylight, they do not reflect the light of oncoming vehicles at night.

By now it must be obvious that one can go to a great deal of trouble, and spend a lot of money on getting properly fitted up for the open road. However, for those with a limited budget, there are a number of practical and cheap alternatives to choose from.

If your bike can be fitted with a small windscreen, it is possible to stay reasonably warm and dry with just a heavy conventional mackintosh. Brand new police macks' can often be obtained for a few pounds and are exceptionally good.

Many professional courier riders will opt for wellington boots in winter: not only are they substantially cheaper than leather boots, but they are completely waterproof, although must be worn with good thick sea socks to keep out the cold and absorb sweat. Hands can be kept dry with thick polythene bags, or even plastic bottles cut in half and painted matt black can make acceptable handle bar muffs. However, as with all aspects of motor cycling, the best costs the most: a proper outfit may not only keep you dry and warm but may well save serious injury or your life in an accident.   SH

Interrupting the Drive

The Clutch performs the function of transmitting the drive progressively, and interrupting the drive whilst gear changing takes place

A CLUTCH HAS LONG BEEN A NECESSITY on a motor cycle for two reasons. First, the internal-combustion engine—unlike the reciprocating steam engine—develops no torque from rest and so has to be run at some speed to propel the machine at all. To get under way from a standstill, therefore, some means has to be provided of enabling the engine to run at a 'working' speed during take-up of the drive. The spring-loaded friction clutch meets this need since it can transmit the drive progressively by being slipped less and less from fully disengaged to fully home.

Second function of the clutch is to interrupt the drive while the rider changes gear. Without such interruption it would be difficult to get out of the gear in use, and to make any engine-speed adjustment to facilitate engagement of the next gear.

Most earlier motor cycles were clutchless; they had single-speed belt transmission and were got on the move by pushing or pedalling. However, once multi-ratio gearboxes came into use, the clutch became an essential feature of the transmission.

Below: the components of a multi-plate clutch assembly from a 250 Suzuki. This is of the coil-spring type. The driving member is the drum on the right of the picture

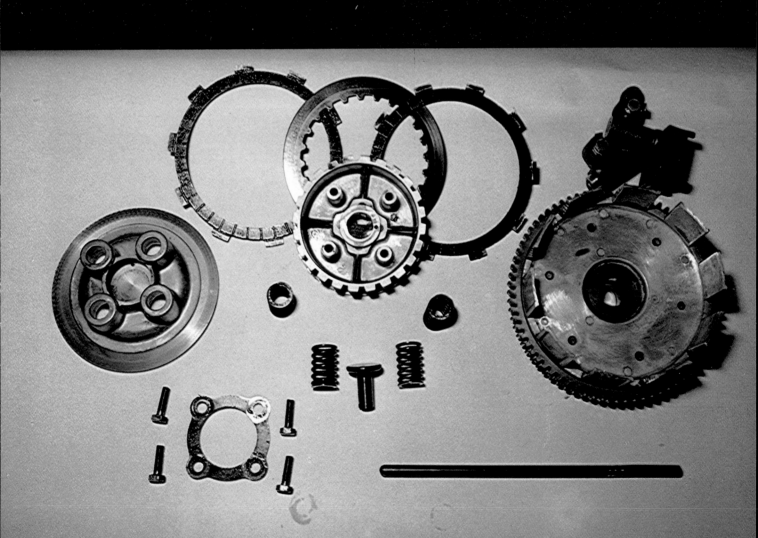

Tony Matthews '77

The friction clutch has changed little in principle since it first appeared, but many improvements have been made through the years to enhance its efficiency and durability. In its simplest form it comprises a driving (or input) member connected to the engine, a driven (or output) member connected to the gearbox, and a spring-loaded pressure-plate; one of the members is usually faced with friction material to increase the grip.

In the engaged condition, the spring-loading clamps the driving and driven members together to transmit the drive. Actuation of the clutch control overcomes the spring thrust and so allows relative rotation between the two members. Conventionally, the control consists of a lever on the left handlebar and a cable connecting it to the clutch release mechanism, but a pedal and linkage system has been employed – notably by Harley-Davidson in the USA.

Although the engine-speed clutch, mounted on the end of the crankshaft, is almost universal on cars, it has never been popular for motor cycles since the high inertia of the rapidly revolving driven member tends to give a poor quality of gearchange. Consequently, clutches of this type are found only on machines with longitudinal crankshafts and no primary reduction in the transmission; where the crankshaft is transverse, the clutch is situated at the gearbox end of the primary drive and so runs more slowly than does the engine.

While this gearing-down facilitates gearchanging, it also increases the torque to be transmitted by the clutch, that torque being the power throughput divided by the speed. In the case of the simple clutch already described, the torque capacity could be increased to obviate unwanted slip merely by stepping-up and spring-loading, but that would multiply the lever effort, maybe to an impossible or very tiring extent.

The multi-plate clutch, which has been in general use for over 50 years, is a more practicable alternative: for a given spring load and effective diameter of the gripping surfaces, the torque capacity increases directly with the number of plates. In a typical multi-plate motor cycle clutch, the driving member is a drum carried on a bearing on the clutch centre; the latter forms an extension of the gearbox input shaft and is the driven member. Earlier practice was for the drum periphery to be interrupted by a series of axial slots which were engaged by projecting tongues on the annular driving plates. Nowadays, however, many clutches have a continuous drum with internal teeth, these being engaged by corresponding teeth on the plates. The driving plates, of either type, carry the friction material on both sides, in the form of rings, discs or segments.

Alternating with the driving plates are the plain driven plates, also annular but with internal tongues or teeth that engage splines or serrations machined on the clutch centre. The spring clamping load is applied through a pressure-plate or cover on the outside of the assembly.

Coil or diaphragm springs

In the vast majority of clutches, axially disposed coil springs – maybe five in number – provide the clamping load. They are housed in thimbles on the back of the pressure-plate and are compressed by abutments screwed on to studs projecting from the back-plate of the drum. The most common release method in this instance is for the lever actuation to move a pushrod housed in the hollow mainshaft of the gearbox; this pushrod in turn moves the pressure-plate against the spring-loading. Because the abutments are adjustable, spring variations can be compensated to ensure square withdrawal of the pressure-plate. Any serious tilting would cause the clutch to 'drag', rather than free fully, to the detriment of the gearchange.

A recent improvement is to replace the multiple coil springs by a single diaphragm spring. This type of spring, fitted to most modern car clutches, has the benefits of simplicity, good rotational balance, uniformity of loading and lower releasing effort for a given clamping force.

Left: a cutaway drawing showing the principal components of a single-plate clutch; from left to right can be seen the flywheel (with starter ring), the driven plate (with splined centre), the pressure plate (with release bearing), the cover (with diaphragm spring and splined output shaft) and the end of the operating rod

Below left: a partially disassembled multi-plate clutch,

showing the plate 'sandwich', the slotted drum and the pressure plate/spring assembly

Below: the same unit in an assembled state, showing how the projections on the driving plates engage in the slots of the driven drum. This is a coil-spring-operated unit, but diaphragm-spring types are now finding wider application

The diaphragm spring is in effect a truncated hollow steel cone sandwiched between two fulcrum rings. Under axial loading from the apex, the cone angle flattens – each radial element pivoting about the rings – and may even be reversed. During assembly of the clutch, the spring is tightened firmly on to the pressure-plate to provide the required preloading; this partially flattens the cone, and the additional release thrust usually takes it beyond the completely flattened state, whereupon the spring rate decreases noticeably.

For light operation, the distance from the central release thrust-ring to the fulcrum rings is made greater than that from the latter to the periphery – i.e. a 'mechanical advantage' is introduced. The release movement is in the opposite direction to that for a coil-spring system, so the mechanism is outboard of the clutch instead of at the remote end of the gearbox.

So far, use of the diaphragm spring appears to have been confined to Norton and Triumph models. In view of its manifold advantages, though, it seems certain to acquire a wider following in the future.

Friction materials

Early motor cycle clutches ran dry (except in the rain!), being protected at best by a sheet-metal cover over the primary chain. Cork was probably the first friction material used on the driving plates but it tended to char under any prolonged slipping, resulting in loss of grip and the need for speedy replacement. Asbestos-based fabrics – not unlike those then employed for brake linings – therefore came into widespread service because of their high resistance to heat.

However, the general adoption of oil bath primary chaincases in the mid-1930s radically altered the clutch's environment. The asbestos facings of those days did not relish a diet of oil, so cork came back into favour; it gave a very sweet action in oil which, cooling as well as lubricating, reduced the liability to charring.

During the course of the history of motor cycles, various manufacturers have adopted metal-to-metal clutches in the search for high resistance to abuse. The best-known examples of this type were the very successful assemblies fitted to post-war racing machines by the Italian Moto-Guzzi concern. They had alternate steel and bronze plates running in oil, and were of quite small diameter for minimal inertia. Owing to the low friction of lubricated metal on metal, however, a lot of plates were necessary, so the clutches were costly. It is worth recording that Kawasaki quite recently adopted a similar layout for their most powerful machines.

Oil had the effect of lowering the coefficient of friction, so more plates or stronger springs were required to maintain the torque capacity. Moreover, the oily plates tended to stick together during spells of idleness; the initial engagement of bottom gear after starting-up was therefore likely to be very scrunchy unless the rider first freed the plates by operating the kickstarter with the clutch lever pulled to the handlebar.

One British manufacturer, Ariel, cleverly sidestepped the oilbath situation for many years by enclosing the clutch in an oiltight cover. Since the plates consequently ran dry, asbestos facings could still be used, so there was no reduction of grip and 'idle sticking' did not occur.

After World War II, some use was made of oil-resistant synthetic rubbers, such as Neoprene, for the frictional duty. They gave adequate grip but were particularly prone to sticking, and they also swelled considerably if the clutch was abused and the facings became overheated. This swelling caused slack to develop in the control cable, so the clutch would not free properly until it cooled down again.

The early 1950s saw the advent of improved cork-base materials comprising granules bonded with synthetic rubber into a sheet. Not only were the strength and frictional properties superior to those of unprocessed cork but – thanks to the latest adhesives – segments or rings cut from the sheet could be stuck securely to the plates. This production method was significantly cheaper than the old one of stamping holes in the plates and pressing-in relatively thick discs or segments which, protruding on both sides, then had to be rubbed down to ensure flatness. Another merit of stuck-on friction elements was better heat dissipation from the rubbing area during slipping of the clutch.

This 'postage stamp' technique quickly became generally adopted, and further advances have since been made in the actual friction materials. Not only have synthetic rubbers or resins become the normal bonding agents but cork has been joined by asbestos and metallic fillers.

Below: an exploded view of the type of clutch most commonly found on motor cycles, the multi-plate assembly. The number, size and friction material of the plates can be varied to suit the power output which the unit is handling in different applications. The components are as listed below

A	adjuster lock nut
B	adjuster screw
C	cap nut
D	center nut
E	inner spring
F	clutch spring
G	hub
H	sliding sleeve
I	pressure plate
J,L,N,P	driving plate
K,M,O	intermediate plate
Q	clutch corks
R	back plate
S	chainwheel assembly
T	primary drive chain
U	ball for roller track
V	chainwheel ball track

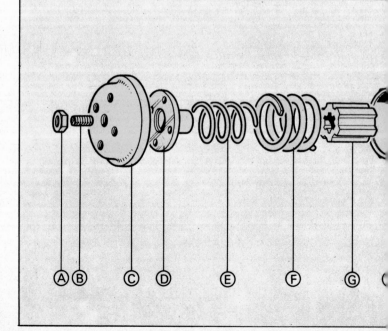

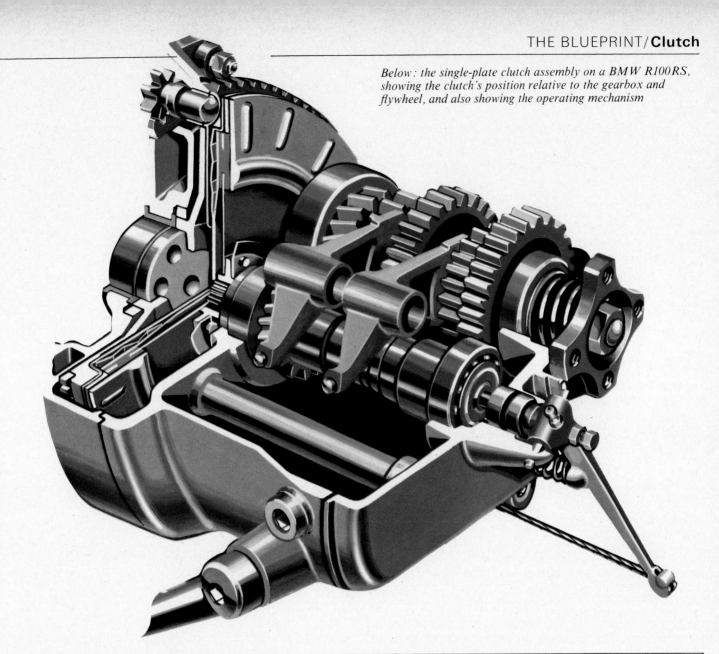

Below: the single-plate clutch assembly on a BMW R100RS, showing the clutch's position relative to the gearbox and flywheel, and also showing the operating mechanism

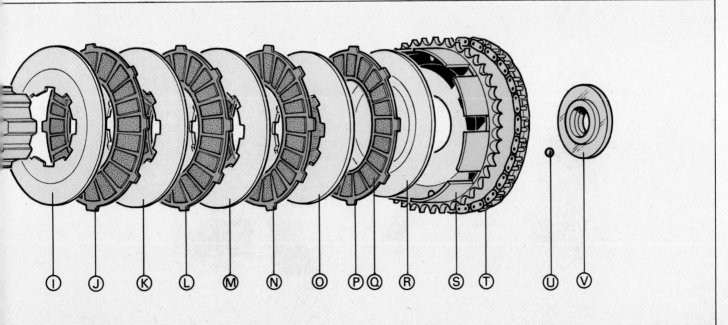

I J K L M N O P Q R S T U V

Automatic clutches

To simplify riding, automatic centrifugal clutches were introduced soon after the war for mopeds and other lightweights; they were best suited to single-speed transmissions because they posed gearchanging problems. The usual arrangement for such a clutch is for the driving member to carry two weighted shoes which are situated within the drum-shape driven member. These shoes are spring-loaded towards the disengaged position, which they maintain at low engine speeds.

As the engine is accelerated, the increasing centrifugal force overcomes the spring-loading and moves the shoes outward into contact with the drum to take up the drive. Clutches of this type work well enough for low-torque drives, but in general they do not have particularly smooth engagement characteristics.

An interesting application of automaticity – (self-servo) to be precise – was to be found in the two-stage clutches fitted to the still-lamented Vincent twin-cylinder motor cycles of the postwar era. Release of the clutch lever engaged a light single-plate 'pilot' clutch; the resultant torque on the driven member of this clutch was used to force the shoes of the main clutch outward into contact with a drum on the driven shaft. A high torque, instead of causing slipping, actually pressed the shoes more firmly on to the drum.   AB

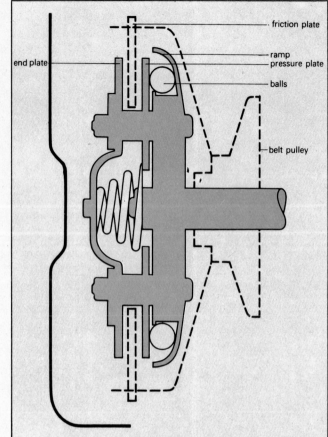

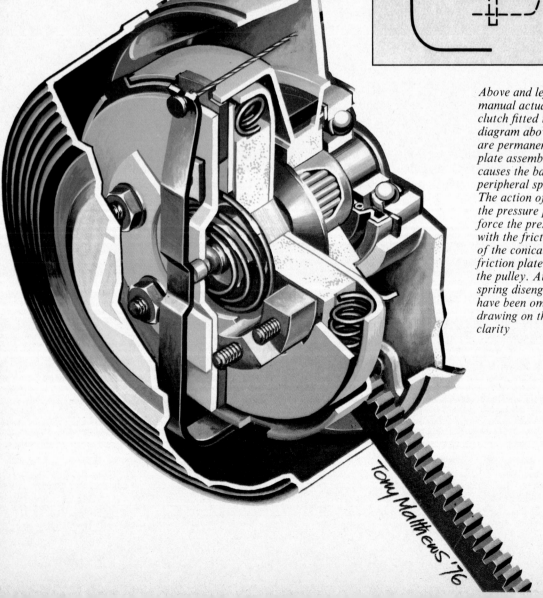

Above and left: not all clutches require manual actuation; this is the automatic clutch fitted to Batavus mopeds. In the diagram above, the parts in solid black are permanently driven; as the driven plate assembly rotates, centrifugal force causes the ball bearings retained in the peripheral spring to be thrown outwards. The action of the balls moving between the pressure plate and the ramp is to force the pressure plate into contact with the friction plate, against the action of the conical spring, sandwiching the friction plate and transmitting drive to the pulley. At idling speeds the conical spring disengages the drive. The balls have been omitted from the cutaway drawing on the left for the sake of clarity

Churchill's Choice

**The Clyno Motor Cycle Company was selected by
Sir Winston Churchill to produce machine-gun
carriers in World War I**

During its twenty year lifespan, the Clyno company was a household name, first in the motor cycle world, and then among makers of mass produced cars. In both fields, it reached the heights and then fell like Icarus.

They used to say that the name Clyno was derived from the phrase a Car Like You've Never Owned, but in fact it went right back to the origins of the company in the first decade of the century, even before it built complete vehicles.

One of the drawbacks of early motor cycles was the inflexibility of their single-ratio belt drives, and various proprietary variable-ratio devices were marketed to save riders from having to pedal uphill too violently. One of the better of these devices was a two-speed pulley invented by two cousins from Thrapston, Northamptonshire, Frank and Alwyn Smith. They called their invention an 'inclined pulley', later abbreviated this to 'Clined', and finally devised the name Clyno. The Clyno Pulley, claimed its young inventors, was capable of being adjusted in five seconds by the hands only and was available with an extension for driving a cooling fan.

By 1909, the cousins had progressed to the construction of a complete motor cycle, although it was assembled from proprietary parts such as Chater-Lea forks and frame fittings and a 5–6hp Stevens engine built in Wolverhampton by the Stevens brothers, who were on the point of launching their own AJS marque after several years of power-plant manufacture.

The Clyno Engineering Company Limited made its exhibition debut in November 1909, at the Stanley Show at the Agricultural Hall, Islington, where the exhibits consisted of the 744cc 5–6hp V-twin and two 3hp models of 386cc; a novel feature of the 3hp singles was that the complete engine/carburettor/magneto/silencer unit could be removed from the frame by unscrewing two bolts. Price of the 3hp model was 39 guineas, while the larger model cost 49 guineas.

Within the next twelve months, Clyno moved from Thrapston into the recently vacated Stevens Screws factory in Pelham Street, Wolverhampton, where the father of their engine suppliers had carried on business as a precision engineer. For a time, Clyno also acted as selling agents for the Stevens engines, the 3hp retailing at £11 and the 5–6hp at £18.

At the 1910 Olympia Motor Cycle Show, Clyno exhibited a new version of the 5–6hp model, fitted with a foot-operated two-speed epicyclic gear, chain final drive and free engine clutch. By the following Show, this new model had become Clyno's sole offering, as the 3hp single had been dropped along with belt drive and the Clyno Patent Pulley. The company seemed to have taken over the

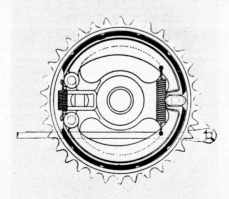

rights to the V-twin Stevens engine, as there was now no longer any mention of this unit's origins and AJS were fitting a 697cc engine to their machines.

Six chain-drive Clynos were shown at Olympia in 1911, and design refinements included the enclosure of valves and final-drive chain in dustproof casings and the option of two or four speeds and a 'foot starting device'. The reason for the latter fitting was that the Clyno was being developed as a sidecar machine, to which end the company had begun to manufacture sidecars of 'Clyno special design, with patent arrangement for two stays to front of machine and two to rear, double suspension of sidecar wheel, magnificent coach-built torpedo body, with spare tyre and carrier. Complete £85 5s. Sidecar can be fitted with wind screen and hood extra'.

Increasingly, the Clyno was becoming a machine designed for comfort and convenience: the 1913 models had three-speed gearing and quickly detachable wheels fore and aft, with the sidecar wheel interchangeable with those on the machine; a pan seat was standard; ample mudguarding allowed for the fitting of 3in section tyres; aluminium footboards were provided for the rider's protection and sidecars were now three-point suspended. In fact, the *tout ensemble* was finished throughout in the very best style. Its colour scheme was 'Clyno special silver grey enamel lined blue; tank grey

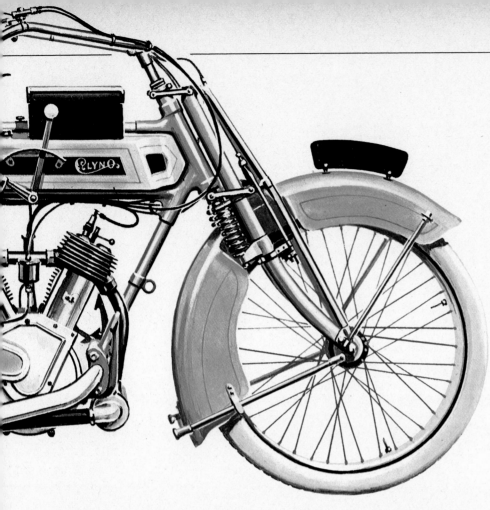

with blue panels lined gold; wheels enamelled grey all over except portion of rim left for front wheel brake; sidecar coachbuilt body painted blue'.

There was a return to the lightweight fold in 1913 with the announcement of a 2½hp baby two-stroke single, but the reputation of Clyno still rested on the old 5–6hp twin. Shortly, this model would be called upon to face hazards which even its manufacturers, who took every opportunity of proving their product's worth in reliability trials, could never have anticipated. For, with the outbreak of war in 1914 came a demand for a heavy motor cycle combination to carry machine guns, and a trial for eligible machines was organised.

Among the entries was an unorthodox tricar designed by Alfred Angas Scott, a design which was to be resurrected in peacetime as the Scott Sociable, but the officer in charge of the trials, one Winston Churchill, rejected this machine in favour of the more conventional Clyno, which by now was fitted with a spring device in the final drive for smoother running.

Orders flowed in for the Clyno outfits and, by 1915, the factory was working eighteen hours a day to meet demand; already, four complete batteries of the Motor Machine Gun Outfit had been equipped with Clynos. Within these batteries, the Clynos operated in units of three: one was armour plated and carried a Vickers machine gun mounted on a detachable tripod on the sidecar chassis; the second was also armoured, but un-armed – the gun was transferred to it in case of emergency – and the third was unarmoured, carrying spare ammunition. The gun carriers were fitted with a box behind the gunner's seat which contained ammunition, water, tools, spares for the gun, petrol, oil and carbide. There was a pillion seat, the wheels were detachable and interchangeable, with a spare carried alongside the pillion; also, large-section Rom tyres were standardised. The riders and gunners were paid 2½d a day all found, plus 6d proficiency pay.

Clyno were building something like 100 of these machine-gun outfits a year, and every weekend during 1915–16, a convoy of Clyno combinations was driven down to Kempton Park, where military machines were marshalled before being shipped over to France. Claude Heckford, Clyno service manager, who joined the company in 1914, recalled that anyone who could ride a motor cycle was 'roped-in' to help with the delivery. 'We had quite a decent convoy . . . they were a thundering good old bike, those were – they would slog on for ever!'.

A new design of motor machine-gun outfit appeared in 1917. This was the 'Russian Eight', powered by an 8hp JAP engine, about 1500 of which were

Left above: a view of the camshaft drive gear with side valves and pushrods of a sidecar outfit as supplied to the Russian army in World War I

Left below: the one leading and one trailing shoe arrangement Clyno brake

Above: a 1913 5–6hp Clyno in solo form; these immaculate machines sold for £79

Below: another 5–6hp machine, this time being a 1912 example complete with matching sidecar. This Clyno was in everyday use right up until 1955

built for the Russian Army, who apparently also took a number of 5–6hp combinations. Instruction books were prepared in Russian for both mdels.

Another wartime venture was a four-cylinder motor cycle combination developed at the request of the War Office. It had an in-line water-cooled power unit and a two-speed epicyclic gearbox. Recalled Ben Browning, who had gone to Clyno in 1915 from Alldays & Onions to work on the design of the 5–6hp motor machine-gun outfit: 'The job was completed, but no order was forthcoming, as the war drew to a close before the job was required. But we put a box sidecar on the machine itself, and ran it round as a commercial job, collecting materials and all that sort of thing. They only made probably three or four four-cylinder machines. These 10hp ohv power units were fitted into prototype light cars as well as the combination'.

Because of the company's proven manufacturing abilities, it was chosen to manufacture a V12 aero engine of Vauxhall design. However, after only two or three prototypes had been completed, this project was dropped, and the decision taken to manufacture the ABC Dragonfly radial aero engine. The aero engine side was under the charge of Charles van Eugen, and started operation at the beginning of 1918; van Eugen designed much of the machinery needed to produce the Dragonfly, a 320hp nine-cylinder engine designed by Granville Bradshaw, while Mr Browning was responsible for making the gauges for its manufacture. 'There was only a few feet between our drawing office and the test-bed,' he remembered, 'so you can imagine the racket that was going on! The aero engine job was given to Clyno and also to Guy, and we had a race to see which could produce the first engine . . . Clyno won!'.

Unfortunately, the race was destined to finish too late. Charles van Eugen told the author: 'The first engine ran on the test bench on Armistice Day, 11 November 1918 . . . and production continued until peace was declared in about July 1919. The contract was cancelled and Frank Smith and his father (chairman of the company) were left holding the baby and they had to revert to motor cycle production. Although I was not interested, I was persuaded to stay on and found myself saddled with being in charge of the jig and tool design office'.

The Smiths had other problems, too, including industrial espionage: 'One of the design staff designed a horizontal-twin machine', said Mr Browning. 'They made the experimental models and then he disposed of the designs to a well known competitor and had the sack through it. A little while later a new machine appeared on the market with a horizontal flat-

twin engine in it!'.

Despite such annoyances, Clyno looked all set to take maximum advantage of the post-war boom in sales. They had a name which had won an excellent reputation during the hostilities – indeed, the exploits of the Motor Machine Gun Service warranted a somewhat ornate War Memorial designed by C. S. Jagger and erected at Hyde Park Corner – and two excellent models in the shape of the 2½hp two-stroke bike in developed form and a new spring-frame 8hp V-twin. However, the changeover to peacetime production took too long. Although the 8hp was shown at the 1919 Motor Cycle Show, the machine was slow to reach the public.

Perhaps the company had scattered its fire, for the design department was working on the development of the 10hp car at this time. Van Eugen was in charge of the project: 'When I returned from my holiday (in the summer of 1920), I found the place upside down; a representative of the money lenders, Thomas de la Rue, had the mainsay and stopped the project and I could not do anything else but carry on with shop equipment design. As I was asked to become works manager of the Briton Motor Company, I left Clyno at the height of the slump and dropped from the frying pan into the fire!'.

For a time, the Clyno factory operated under the manager put in by de la Rue, and the 8hp began to reach the customers. Press enthusiasm was keen: 'Nature decrees that we desire most earnestly the unattainable', commented *The Motor*

Cycle. 'For this reason, close interest in the 8hp Clyno has been and is intense, and now that deliveries are definitely commencing, the interest, by reason of the sheer completeness of the design, will not flag. Of Clyno manufacture and design, the engine has detachable cylinder heads and a carefully planned system of mechanical lubrication . . . the spring frame is simplicity itself, and includes the carrier in its total of sprung weight. Detachable and interchangeable wheels naturally find a place in the standard specification; removal of the rear wheel leaves the internal expanding rear brake in situ, also of course the transmission. Mudguarding is literally on car lines, and to car dimensions. The *modele de luxe* has full electrical equipment, but even the standard machine is exceptionally complete. War and peace have provided experience and testing grounds for the Clyno designers, of which they have not been slow to take advantage.'

However, the 8hp never got into full production. In 1922, the Clyno Engineering Company was reformed, to concentrate – very successfully – on building a Coventry Climax-engined light car. Motor cycles were still assembled from spares on hand but, by August 1923, the 'almost phenomenal growth' of car production caused two-wheeler manufacture to be 'suspended indefinitely' – which in Clyno's case meant for ever .   DBW

Below: a family outing with a sidecar outfit in Northern Ireland just before World War I

Quiet, modest, shy even, Peter Collins off the track certainly looks the character usually described as 'that nice young man who lives round the corner'. So he is, too. However, for those who live in the Lymm neighbourhood of Cheshire, and to the hundreds of thousands of speedway fans throughout the world, he is much more than that: he is Peter Collins, World Champion.

For, at the magnificent Slaski Stadium at Chorzow, Katowice, in Poland in September 1976 before a huge 100,000 crowd, he trounced the fifteen strong opposition (an American, an Australian, a Czech, a New Zealander, a West German, two Russians and four riders each from England and the hosts, Poland) to reach the pinnacle of his short speedway career: his first world championship title. It was a triumphant day for England and particularly memorable for the 2500 ardent British enthusiasts present.

22 years old when he won the crown, Collins' fine achievement marked the first English victory for fourteen years, and only the fourth English win in 31 finals altogether, dominated in the past by riders from New Zealand and Sweden.

Born on 24 March 1954, in Manchester, Collins riding a motor cycle is like a dolphin in the sea – he is a natural. The eldest of six children – five brothers and a sister – his earliest experience was gleaned hammering a 98cc Villiers, followed by 'bitsa' BSAs and Triumph Tiger Cubs, around the fields of the family farm near Lymm: fun and games were also practised with a now famous pair of speedway brothers, the Mortons, Chris and Dave. The second eldest Collins, Leslie, after a successful 1976 season riding for Stoke in the National League, moved up to join his famous brother in the Belle Vue team for 1977.

It was watching Belle Vue as a seven-year-old fan that first sparked off Peter's enthusiasm to compete. Eligible to race at sixteen, his first competition was a grass track event and he met with instantaneous success by winning his first race. Nearby Frodsham enthusiast, Jim Rowlinson, the first to predict that Peter would one day become World Champion, took him under his wing and provided sponsorship for the next season. On his bikes, Peter won the British 350cc grass track championship in 1971 at 17, the youngest grass champion ever. That

Right: Peter Collins seen hard at work at a grass-track meeting at Lydden Hill in Kent. On grass or cinders, Peter shines and is usually the man to beat

World Champion of the Cinders

It took Peter Collins only five years to progress from British Grass Track Champion to 1976 World Speedway Champion

success was repeated the following season supported by second places in the 250cc and 500cc championships. His first days on shale came in 1971 and, seeing his potential, Peter was signed up by Belle Vue and loaned out to get experience with the next door club, Rochdale, the home of the Hornets.

His rapid rise to fame swept all before him with an average 9.80 points out of a possible 12 at the end of the season with the Hornets; also he managed a 6.36 average for a shorter Belle Vue Aces racing programme. A reserved personality, the dark, curly, brown-haired youngster may have been, but once on a bike he changed to a

demon with a passion for speed.

As iron filings are drawn to a magnet, so his spectacular, full-throttle, give-the-bike-its-head style attracts admiration and respect from other riders, admirers and the fans.

If he does have a weak spot it is his starting or, more so, producing consistently fast starts from the tapes which is so important in speedway. For vitally important races, however, he always seems to be able to muster that little extra from his efforts and save the day.

It is Collins' ability to come from the back and win even against the toughest opposition that typifies his races, for it is the sight of someone in front that

Opposite page: Peter Collins awaits the start of a race on his 500cc Jawa

Below: Peter Collins riding for England during an international meeting in 1975

Below right: Peter's other success of 1976 was marrying his attractive girl-friend, Angela, and the pair are pictured here after the World Final in Poland

urges him on to produce his own magical skills of balance, control, trackcraft and rip-roaring pace that thrills the crowds.

Fourth in the BBC Sports Personality of the Year competition, preceded by third in the *Daily Express* Sportsman of the Year event, are proof of his growing recognition and public popularity over the last few months of 1976.

However, back to his career. He built himself up to number one at the Aces over the next two to three seasons, winning the British Junior Champion title in 1973 and undertaking two long and highly successful trips with British Lions tours of Australia.

Peter was capped for Young England in his speedway debut year, 1971, and represented the full England team for many years. He shined for his country, too, in World Team Cup events with a maximum 12 points for the Great Britain team in the Wembley final in 1973, 12 again the next season for the succeeding England side in Poland, and, to cap it all, another maximum in the Norden, West Germany, final in 1975.

These were performances unrivalled by anyone, anywhere, in that world championship. Although he was twelfth in his first individual world final with 6 points in 1973, the following year he moved up to sixth in the world scoring 9 points in Sweden. In the build up to the final that year, he won an exciting run-off for the title of European Champion, beating former world champions Ole Olsen and Ivan Mauger – it was the first significant title held by an Englishman since the later Peter Craven won the world crown in 1962.

The tight-cornered Wembley track, which had witnessed so many of his triumphs, looked his best chance of gaining world honours in 1975. Two race wins set him on his way but then a disastrous third race, when he finished last, quashed his early strong challenge. Ole Olsen rode superbly for his second world title on a dusty, bumpy and strongly criticised track.

Unbeaten in 1974 and 1975, it was the stylish Olsen again, riding the new and more potent four-valve Jawa, who Collins prevented from repeating his World Team Cup record in the British League Division One Riders' Championship in 1976.

You cannot win them all – one big omission in his list of victories is the British championship – but certainly Collins has the skill, determination and aptitude, with the delightful knack of setting and extending new records in the sport; he is a worthy world champion.

To make a fairytale ending to 1976, he also won another victory of sorts off the track – he married fiancée Angela Hilton in November.   SB

FIRE POWER

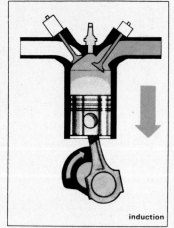
induction

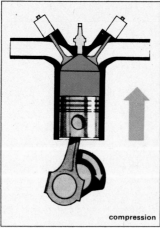
compression

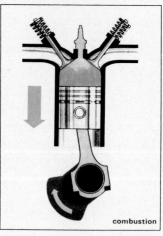
combustion

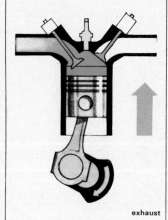
exhaust

WHEN AN ENGINE is running, there is an inferno within each cylinder, an inferno that liberates the energy stored in the fuel. It is a pent-up fire that is rigorously controlled, yet one that accomplishes its task far more swiftly than the layman might think possible and more swiftly than even some theoreticians think proper. In fact, it is not fully understood even by those scientists who have come to terms with its apparent disobedience of the rules, and who have studied its processes for generations in the hope of finding a new source of efficiency in fuel utilisation. Great advances have been made in this field, especially with the advent of emission-control regulations, but there is still a considerable amount to learn.

The strangest of all phenomena associated with the internal combustion engine is the actual combustion, the process by which petrol is burned in air to generate hot high-pressure gases that may then be expanded by the piston moving down-

wards and the energy thus liberated turned to useful work. There is no mystery about the fuels: most of the common ones are hydrocarbons (such as petrol), matching the generalised formula C_xH_y, but there are also fuels of organic origin (alcohol, for instance) that carry a little oxygen with them and are of the form $C_xH_yO_z$. The energy content of a fuel is usually known pretty precisely – there are some 10,550 Chu (Celsius heat units) or 19,000 Btu in a pound of petrol, for example – and even after making allowances for the loss of some of this calorific content because of the latent heat of evaporation of the fuel itself, it should still be fairly straightforward to work out just what should be happening when a spark leaps the plug gap to ignite it. We could forecast that the carbon and hydrogen of the fuel would combine with the oxygen of the air to produce a calculable heat, plus oxides of carbon (CO or CO_2) and hydrogen (H_2O – water, hence the steam in your exhaust after

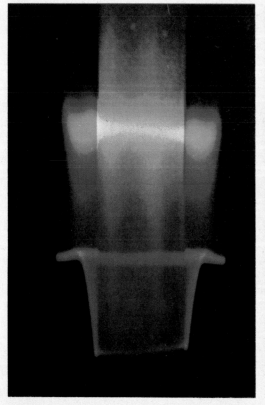

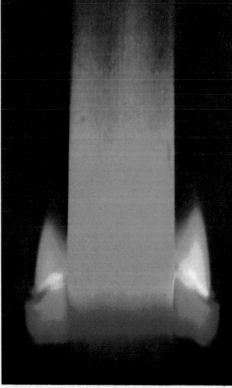

Top: the four sequences of the combustion process

Left: these photographs were taken inside a special test reactor in Milan. The red central portion is a column containing an electric heating element, and this is contained within a larger column. A temperature gradient is set up, starting from cold at the bottom and becoming steadily hotter higher up. A mixture of fuel, oxygen and nitrogen is passed up the space between the two columns and ignition takes place when the mixture is sufficiently heated. The left-hand picture shows an annular blue flame and a chalice-shaped cold flame. The latter occurs at low temperature and is not visible to the naked eye and accounts for the fraction of time the combustion process is in incubation. The right-hand picture shows how the blue flame turns yellow when the fuel/air mixture is enriched.

Right: the Precision vee-twin engine of 1913 with its unconventional combustion chamber design. The combustion chamber is, in fact, of larger diameter than the cylinder bore so a lot of the combustion force will be wasted

Left: a typical two-stroke combustion chamber, with the spark plug in the centre of a part-spherical space; in many cases, the piston has a raised, shaped crown, which fits into part of the combustion chamber to induce turbulence, hence good fuel/air mixing and even, steady combustion; this head is from a Honda CR125 Elsinore

Above: the cylinder head from a Honda CG125, showing the inclined valves in a part-spherical combustion chamber; in this case, the valves are pushrod operated, via rockers, and the inclined layout of the valves improves gas flow and combustion (the latter due to the part-spherical chamber being made possible)

Left: one of the cylinder heads from a Honda GL1000 'Goldwing', which has a water-cooled, horizontally opposed four cylinder engine; the valves are operated, via rockers, from a single overhead camshaft and, once again, the combustion chambers are part spherical with the valves inclined; the difference between this and the single-cylinder unit is that the valves are offset in the chambers, something which allows for larger valves than would otherwise be possible

a cold morning start) and even perhaps some oxides of the nitrogen which is a major constituent of the air and is supposed to be inert, serving only to slow the combustion process.

In fact what happens is far more complex. A chain reaction takes place, analogous to the chain reaction in an atomic bomb: the chemical combination of the different elements liberates others which are free to combine with whatever they can find, when they in turn liberate others to do the same. Thus what starts as a tiny hair-thin flame between the plug points, grows at an ever-increasing rate to fill the whole combustion chamber, as these chain carriers help to carry the reaction to completion. These chain carriers may be ions of gases such as hydrogen or oxygen, free radicals (like OH, CHO, CH etc), or even organic compounds such as HCHO, which is formaldehyde. They may exist only for an instant before destruction; or they may be frozen into permanence by some adverse condition (excessive quenching by over-cooled cylinder walls, for instance) and emerge as some possibly noxious matter in the exhaust gases.

These chain reactions occur within the flame front that moves outwards from the point of ignition, to pass through all the compressed charge within the chamber. How fast it moves, and in what directions, will depend on the design of the engine and the conditions in which it is working. Turbulence has the most marked effect on flame speed, which is why engines can operate at such high cyclic rates: the faster the piston comes up to compress the charge, and the faster that charge is squeezed and squished into its final shape for ignition, and indeed the faster it flows in through the inlet valve during the preceding stroke, the greater will be the turbulence, and the faster the flame travel. This is why no more ignition advance may be needed at 6000rpm than at 4000, say, despite the fact that each combustion may then have to be completed in only two-thirds of the time available at the slower speed. On the other hand, too much turbulence (especially if induced before the inlet valve closes) can have bad results on heat loss and the overall efficiency of an engine.

Mixture strength also has a profound effect. The stoichiometric or 'chemically correct' mixture, ideal for complete and efficient combustion of all the fuel in the charge, is about 14.75:1 by weight of air and petrol respectively; but the mix-

Below: photographs of piston crowns in different conditions; the normal one (left) shows no signs of detonation, while the centre one has had the deposits scoured off its centre by uncontrolled explosions at low speed; high-speed use in the same circumstances will eventually lead to a hole being knocked in the piston crown (right)

ture that gives the highest power output (about 12:1, which gives about 4% more power), does so because the flame travels through it about 17% faster. Really extreme mixtures, such as the very rich 8:1 or the very weak 20:1, slow the flame so much that the engine runs very badly. Transgress these limits very slightly and suddenly the engine will not run at all, for the flame will not be able to move fast enough to sustain itself.

Many other things affect combustion. Atmospheric humidity, the size of the cylinder bore, the timing of the ignition, the position of the spark plug, the velocity of the fresh charge through the inlet port, the presence of hot spots in the combustion chamber (either permanent, such as the exhaust valve, or temporary, such as deposits of ash, carbon and other materials on the piston crown and other surfaces), the amount of end gas remaining to dilute the incoming charge after closure of the exhaust port, and the introduction of lubricating oil past the piston rings or through the valve guides: all these can matter. Other than the timing of the spark, perhaps no other factor is as important as the shape of the combustion chamber: this determines the path and distance of the flame travel, and governs the probability of abnormal ignition taking place with a given fuel if too high a compression ratio is used in the engine.

The greater the compression, then the more rapid and complete is combustion, and the more efficiently can the liberated energy of the fuel be harnessed during the expansion phase. If the compression ratio is too high for a given fuel, however, detonation may occur. Part of the compressed charge trapped in a corner of the combustion chamber may be compressed further by the expansion of the burning gases away from the spark plug, until it ignites spontaneously before the flame front reaches it. Apart from causing objectionable noise and overloading mechanical components, this explosive detonation can make the plug points overheat, or make surface deposits grow incandescent; these then cause pre-ignition of the fresh charge before the spark occurs, with all the destructive consequences that occur when the ignition is too far advanced, or when too soft a spark plug is fitted to the engine. A hole burned in the piston crown is a frequent result, and complete collapse of the piston may take place in a few seconds if this form of abnormal combustion continues. It usually happens during full-load running with too soft or hot a plug, too weak a mixture, or with a fuel too low in its anti-knock (octane) rating, or the spark too far advanced. Slogging up a hill at low engine speed in too high a gear is as likely to produce these results as flat-out motorway driving, where the load may not, in fact, be as great.

In fact, the forms of abnormal ignition may be slightly different in these two cases, but to delve into the differences would involve very lengthy examination of the whole subject of combustion and fuels. Perhaps it is sufficient to recognise, and be grateful for the fact, that the burning of a little petrol in a fair measure of air, such as might occupy a tenth of a second when the mixture is lightly compressed in a static closed vessel, can be controlled to occupy less than a hundredth of a second in a touring-bike engine being driven gently, or less than a thousandth of a second in a racing motor cycle engine at peak power. LJKS

Right: the top pair of drawings shows the spread of the flame front at 4500rpm with regular fuel and with premium fuel. In the lower one, where the premium fuel is used, the front travels fairly slowly away from the spark plug (red star), so normal combustion takes place; in the top one, however, the flame reaches the far side of the chamber in a shorter time (the figures represent milliseconds) and detonation takes place. The lower pair of drawings shows the same process occurring at 5500rpm. Note how much more quickly the flame travels under these conditions.

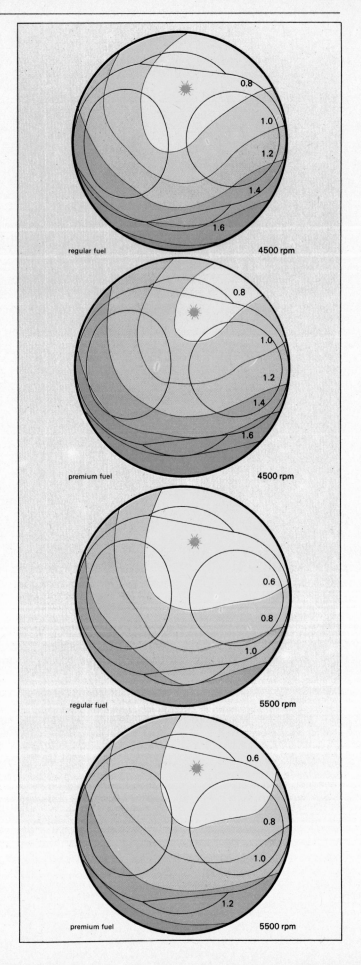

DELIVERING THE GOODS

Compared with four-wheeled machines, motor cycles in a commercial context offer the significant advantages of small size, economy, manoeuvrability and speed in town traffic, and all nicely countered by their inability to carry much in the way of goods! If a sidecar or box with a third wheel is attached to the motor bike, load-carrying capacity is usefully increased but whipping through traffic jams becomes a thing of the past. Years ago, before World War II, the motor cycle and box was a familiar sight on English roads. Milk deliveries, for instance, were mainly by bike, Dunelts being the favoured machine. Sidecar

manufacturers turned out commercial boxes with special fittings for individual concerns with Watsonian, the chief independent maker, still listing such devices as late as the 1940s. In the Midlands in the mid 20s, an enterprising bakery chain equipped roundsmen with 500cc Rudges (wedge tank, four overhead valves, four speeds) lugging not only a trade box but a trailer. Doctors used sidecars as did commercial travellers, plumbers and builders in their small ways. Only in the 1930s with the coming of the small van, based on the newly introduced Austin 7 and Morris 8, did the sidecar box begin to fade from the scene.

In the past few years, motor cycles, with the advent of the despatch-rider services, have made something of a comeback in the commercial field, and few people in London will be unaware of them. Walking, motoring or motor cycling, it can be a nerve-shattering experience to be overtaken by a disembodied voice, of necessity loud enough to cut through exhaust din and layers of full-face helmeting, issuing from a speeding motor cycle plastered with a name like Delta or Mercury or Hermes or Road Runner or Pony Express or Inter-City Courier. The riders are young, ride well, if forcefully, and their numbers seem to be increasing.

The heart of any despatch rider organisation is a control staff working with a large-scale map of the area they are covering and transmitting radioed instructions to the riders; In big cities it is easy to understand the mushrooming success of the firms in the business when taking into account soaring postal charges and the like.

Above: a Royal Automobile Club outfit followed by the vehicle which was to render it obsolete.

303

Once upon a long time ago, a man in blue on a motor bike was not by definition a policeman. He might have been an RAC patrolman whose job was to help, not to book, you. At the beginning indeed he might, with the tacit approval of his superiors, have conspired to help you against 'them' by giving an unobtrusive signal (or, doubly subtle, by *not* giving the mandatory to-members-only, salute) to warn of some impending police trap. The RAC patrolman, and his much more numerous Automobile Association counterpart, was driving a motor cycle and box filled with get-you-home gadgetry. The AA was first in the field, with some of their Superintendents being elevated from pedal cycles to motor bikes in 1909, a more general swing taking place ten years later with the purchase by the AA of 12 2½hp Chater Lea machines fitted with box sidecars. By 1923, there were no fewer than 270 RSOs (Road Service Outfits) – all BSAs – on the road, rising to 1000 by the late 1930s. The force swelled to a peak of

1800 in 1952, all with radio-to-base communication. It represented pretty big business and prestige for BSA, Britain's biggest motor cycle and sidecar maker, and all seemed set fair . . . until the arrival of the Mini at the end of the 50s offering more capacity, relative comfort for the patrolman and, probably, lower running costs (600cc side-valve motors tugging up to a half-ton of irregularly shaped hardware through rarely tranquil British air being even more notable for thirst than for their lack of performance). In 1963, the decision was made to replace the AA outfit over a five-year phase-out and on 1 April 1968, the last fifteen outfits had a 'drive past' final parade. A flicker of interest in the motor cycle recurred in July 1972 when the AA took on four solos, 650 Triumphs this time, to work in London, rising to nine a year later, later augmented by a couple in the Midlands and Scotland.

At the Royal Automobile Club, always reckoned to have the interests of the motor cyclist more firmly at heart than the rival camp, the scale of operations was much smaller, however, with the 16H Norton – a side-valve like the AA's BSA but smaller, at 490cc, and livelier (if such a word, even in a comparative sense, may be used of a 17bhp all-iron side-valve) being introduced in 1928 to replace earlier Ivy machines. The most motor cycle patrols used by the RAC was 400 and, as with the AA, the minivan killed them in the 60s.

The mini van can doubtless take some credit for (metaphorically) killing off the motor cycle-mounted telegram boy, surely in his time one of the speediest combinations of man and machine to be encountered in city traffic and narrow

Above: seen on UK roads for many years were the Automobile Association outfits

Opposite page: a familiar sight in most large cities, the despatch rider

Top: these three-wheeled Vespa Tri-Vans are very common in Italy and are used in place of more conventional four-wheeled vehicles. Power comes from a motor-scooter engine

country lanes. Much more pointed reasons, of course, are the ease of telephoning now, the escalation in telegram charges and (for business) an extending use of telex. The Post Office introduce a pious note by adding that they (the PO), would not send out motor cycle boys in bad weather – we use post vans then'. Another factor which might be thought to have influenced the GPO towards its belief that telegram boys on motor cycles were not part of the corporation's image for the 1970s was the fade-out in production of the BSA Bantam, staple motor bike for the job.

Now, the GPO parcels up its little red Bantams for auction (in 1977, there are only about 130 left in service) and restricts its two-wheeler interests to a substantial number of mopeds, with more than 1000 of them, mainly Austrian Puch machines, employed on telegraph business.

At one time, most motor cycle traders sported a sidecar float comprising a scruffy but powerful bike (once a big vee twin, latterly a vertical twin 650) in loose-limbed company with a third wheel, with between them some oily planks on which to support one or more roped-down motor bikes. These floats, sometimes proclaiming the dealer's name but often sensibly not, were much used in days when the motor cycle trade was interested in the secondhand market and thought it worthwhile to collect machines from private vendors and auctions. The driver would be the youngest on the dealer's payroll whose services in the workshop would be regarded as happily expendible. Sometimes equally unskilled as a sidecar pilot, or worse, possessed of a certain flair, lightning reflexes and a burning ambition to set standard time over a familiar route, his progress through and around rush-hour traffic was a pheno-

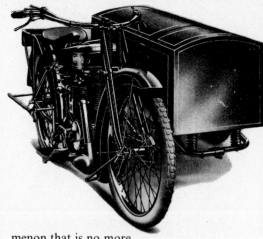

menon that is no more.

The motor cycle as a 'commercial' vehicle? How far can 'commercial' be stretched? Motor cycles are to be seen just ahead of some racing pedal cyclists, pacing them, at Midlands velo dromes and just behind and generally around other racing cyclists performing in other events.

If you have ever been cut up by a vaguely official looking chap riding a 500 Honda with some verve it will be of passing interest to learn that he may be employed by the BBC and that his Honda is one of 12 500s maintained by the Corporation.

There has yet, however, to be a pensioning off for British sheep dogs following a precedent set in Australia with Suzuki trail bikes!　　CA

Left: a Post Office despatch rider astride a BSA Bantam at Twickenham sorting office, about to make a telegram delivery

Top: Chater Lea's 4¼hp Commercial Sidecar model of 1925

Below: a Merryweather fire tender coupled to a Triumph motor cycle in 1913

Packing the Punch

From top dead centre, after the initiation of combustion, to the moment of effective opening of the exhaust port, is the phase of the petrol engine's operating cycle when the burnt or burning charge inside the cylinder is allowed to expand. In the thermodynamic cycle which governs the operation of the internal combustion engine, this expansion phase is the one in which useful (that is, power productive) work is done. The greater the expansion ratio, the greater the amount of energy that can be extracted from the burning charge. Since the expansion phase begins when the piston is at the top of its stroke, it follows that the smaller the combustion chamber volume remaining above it, the greater the expansion ratio will be.

If the expansion ratio is so important, why do we always talk and think in terms of the compression ratio? The answer is that it is more easily measured, more easily felt, makes its own contribution to (and imposes its own limits on) engine performance, and is usually the same as the expansion ratio anyway. There might be a slight difference introduced by asymmetric valve timing, but otherwise there is none in any motor cycle engine: hyperexpansion engines have been built, in which the expansion ratio is much greater than the compression ratio, but they are rare and stationary monsters, unsuitable for vehicle propulsion.

Expansion follows compression of the charge to prepare it for combustion. The greater the compression the better, within limits; but knowing where those limits lie is another matter, approached through an appreciation of what the compression ratio is and means.

The term is simply a numerical expression of the extent to which the charge of fuel and air mixture, drawn into an internal combustion engine, is compressed before expansion. In the conventional piston engine, it is the ratio of the volume of the cylinder and its combustion chamber when the piston is at the bottom of its stroke to the volume remaining when the piston is at the top of its stroke. The smaller the remaining combustion space then is, the higher will the compression ratio be.

The higher the compression ratio of a given engine, the greater is the net power that it will then develop – provided that the compression is not so great as to induce the charge to detonate instead of burning smoothly and progressively as it should. Moreover, the improvement in combustion caused by increasing the compression – which heats the charge and improves its homogeneity – allows more efficient utilisation of the heat energy in the fuel during the expansion phase, so for a given power output the high-compression engine will consume less fuel.

Unfortunately, the relationship between compression ratio and thermal efficiency is not governed by any simple law capable of straightforward mathematical statement; but an illustration of the effect can be given from results obtained with a laboratory test engine run at its most economical mixture setting. At a compression ratio of 4:1, its specific fuel consumption was 0.55 pounds of fuel per horsepower per hour; at 5:1 the fuel consumption figure dropped to 0.485lb/hph; at 6:1 to 0.445; at 7:1 to 0.420lb/hph.

Below: the relationship between the combustion volume with the piston at bottom dead centre (x) and the volume with the piston at top dead centre (y) can be expressed as the compression ratio—$\dfrac{x}{y}$

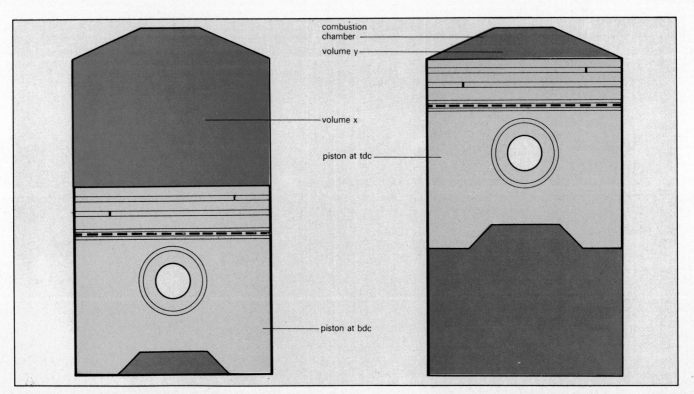

Such figures might represent the limit for one engine, or be only the beginning for another. In a given engine, the limit to compression is imposed by the tendency of the fuel to detonate: the use of a fuel having higher anti-knock or non-detonating properties (that is, in popular language, a higher octane value) will allow the compression ratio to be raised further. A typical engine might be limited by 70-octane petrol to a compression ratio of 5.5:1, but feed it with 90-octane fuel and its compression ratio could be raised to 7:1, or to 9:1 with 98-octane fuel.

There is nothing to be gained by using high-octane fuel if the compression ratio is not high enough to exploit it: there is no point whatever in feeding four-star petrol to a new machine designed to run on two star. When that engine has seen considerable service, then its octane requirement may rise, due to deposits formed within the cylinder head – not because of their effect on the compression ratio, which will be negligible, but because they can incandesce or otherwise promote detonation or pre-ignition. On the other hand, if the compression ratio be raised appropriately to complement a higher-grade fuel, then the greater thermal efficiency derived from the higher compression and expansion ratios will be revealed not only in lower specific fuel consumption but also in greater power output. By raising the compression to exploit 90-octane fuel instead of 70, the power will be augmented by about 20 per cent: raise it to perhaps 9.25:1 to justify 100-octane fuel, and the power will be about 40 per cent higher than on 70-octane; on fuel equivalent to 110-octane, a ratio somewhat in excess of 12:1 might yield power 90 per cent higher than on 70-octane at 5.5:1.

Apart from the properties of the fuel, there are many other factors serving to limit compression ratio. One is the greater mechanical loads imposed on pistons, connecting rods, big-end and main bearings, and other stressed parts, by the higher peak pressures realised during combustion. More difficult to overcome are the problems of combining a combustion chamber of good shape and small enough size with valves large enough to pass the required amounts of charge and exhaust gas. It is necessary for good and efficient combustion that the shape of the space in which it takes place – the volume above the piston at the top of its stroke – should have the greatest possible ratio of volume to surface area, and in modern engines it has usually been this, rather than fuel qualities, that has governed the maximum compression ratio.

The introduction of legislation concerned with exhaust emissions has changed the situation somewhat. It is a combination of high pressure and high temperature that encourages the formation, during combustion, of the oxides of nitrogen that the new laws have sought to reduce, and those conditions are produced in high-compression engines. Accordingly, there has been a move to lower compression ratios, further encouraged by popular misgivings about the lead compounds added as knock-inhibitors to high-octane fuels: low-lead petrol requires a low compression ratio because it is usually of relatively low octane rating. At the other extreme, alcohol fuels permit exceptionally high compression ratios, because they are slow to burn, have a high octane rating, and they need no lead compounds.

An alternative means of increasing the compression is to compress the charge before it is delivered to the cylinder, and this can be done with some form of supercharging pump. The effect on the engine's character and performance is quite different, because the expansion ratio remains unaffected. Further expansion of the exhaust gases into a turbine may allow more energy to be harnessed: the turbocharger is widely acclaimed as a good means of achieving this. However, since forced induction is at present hardly suitable for roadgoing motor cycles, and since supercharging has been prohibited in racing since the late 1940s, the sole application of these techniques is currently limited to sprinting competition.

More relevant to the motor cycling scene is a convention sometimes (but not at all consistently) applied to the measurement of compression ratio in two-stroke engines. Those who observe this convention do not measure the volume above the piston when it is at the bottom of its stroke, as a starting-point for their calculations: instead, they measure the volume above it at the point where it has risen far enough to shut off all the ports that it controls in the cylinder walls. Apparently low compression ratios should therefore be regarded with some suspicion in the specifications of two-stroke engines: the difference may be as between 7:1 and 10:1. If this convention were to be applied consistently, it would have to be used for four-stroke engines, too, measuring the volume above the piston at the moment of inlet valve closure (which is a lot later than bottom dead centre) and relating this to the volume of the fully compressed charge. Whatever the rights and wrongs of the idea, it is most unlikely to enjoy general acceptance from experienced motor cyclists. LJKS

Below: there is an empirical relationship between the compression ratio and the thermal efficiency of an engine. In theory the maximum efficiency would be obtained at a compression ratio of around 15:1 but with pump fuel the onset of detonation limits the usable ratio well below 15:1

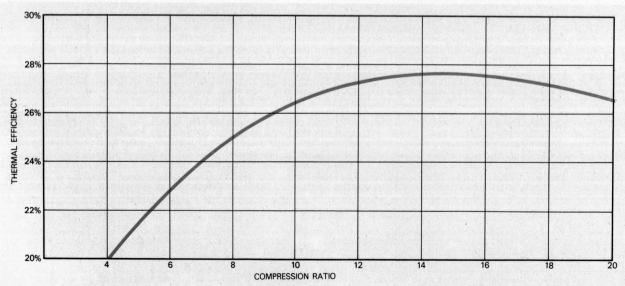

From End to End

Joining piston to crankshaft, the connecting rod's small end bearing fits the piston's gudgeon pin, and the big end bears on the crankshaft

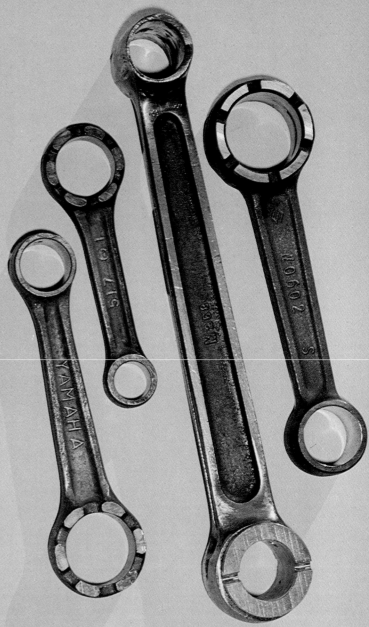

The conventions of engine construction (comprising piston, connecting rod, crankshaft and crankcase as the architectural essentials) were established as long ago as 1780 and have since been more supported by convenience than by authority, their invention having been patented by one James Pickard, a Birmingham button maker. As he arranged things, so the manufacturers of motor cycle power units have been content to arrange them ever since, with but few Wankels and other revolutionaries crying in the wilderness. Thus, while the motion of an engine's piston is strictly linear, that of the crankshaft is rotational; so that of the connecting rod (commonly abbreviated as con-rod or conrod) which links them is translatory. At the little end, the motion of the rod is in a straight line, but at the big end the motion is circular – and it is all very unfortunate, for this swinging action of the conrod is responsible for many of the piston engine's problems. Vibrations, bearing restrictions, difficulties in breathing and burning, even ignition and valve timing, are all sensitive to the proportions of this vital link.

In its construction, the con-rod has few mysteries. The little end (the bearing eye in which the piston's gudgeon pin is a very precise fit) has its dimensions more or less fixed by piston design. The big end (the portion which bears on the crankshaft) is usually split for convenience in manufacture and assembly, for the stronger and lighter one-piece rod demands the expense of a built-up crankshaft. There is a conflict of ideals involved in settling this very basic choice: the one-piece rod is better than the split rod, but a one-piece crankshaft is usually better than a built-up one, notably in its stiffness. So long as the conventional motor cycle engine had only one cylinder or, failing that, was a simple V-twin, a built-up crankshaft could be made amply stiff, and was actually cheaper than a one-piece forging in those days when metallurgy had not yet given us irons suitable for casting such a component. Today, beam and torsional stiffness requirements make a built-up crankshaft undesirable, and it is only adopted when the designer feels convinced of the desirability of observing the roller-bearing usage that is likewise a motor cycling tradition.

Rolling-element bearings for the main journals of the crankshaft are all very well; but their use as big-end bearings (which is what encourages the use of the one-piece rod) is erroneous, because the angular swing of the con rod as it moves makes the rollers skid and wear rapidly. Only in the more rudimentary of two-stroke engines (the only two-strokes found in motor cycles) where the crankcase is washed with

Above right: variations on a theme; from left to right, conrods from an RD250 Yamaha, an FS1-E Yamaha, a 1910 Premier and a Suzuki 250 single. The length of the rod has a special significance as outlined below

Inset: with the same stroke in each case, con-rod angularity varies in relation to the rod's length

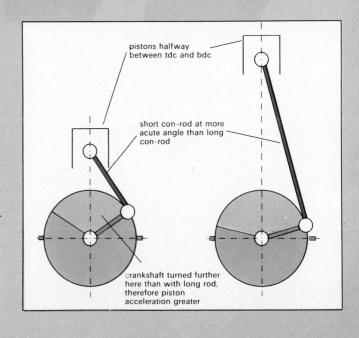

pistons halfway between tdc and bdc

short con-rod at more acute angle than long con-rod

crankshaft turned further here than with long rod, therefore piston acceleration greater

draughts of petrol and air, is the roller bearing a necessary evil. In fact, there is no need to associate the plain bearing with a split big-end eye; but if it is to be split, there are preferred ways of doing it. First, the split line should be perpendicular to the main axis of the rod, and in motor cycle practice this is usually so. Secondly, the faces to be mated at the split should be serrated rather than flat (and this requirement is less commonly met) in order not only to ensure true alignment of the bolt holes and preserve the bolts (or studs) from shear, but also to increase the mating area through which heat may be transferred from rod to cap, and also to reduce the danger of fretting corrosion between the mating surfaces. More important is the danger of the rod being weakened by the machined flat or counterbore which may locate the D-shaped heads of the bolts: these cause sudden changes in section that act as stress-raisers in what is already a very highly stressed area.

As for the shank between big and little ends, few designers bother to make it other than in the H-section which is easiest to forge. For a given cross-sectional area of metal (and therefore a given weight), the H-section beam is obviously stiffer than a symmetrically solid bar. Equally obviously, a tubular shank would be stiffer still, and such rods were once looked upon with favour; however, the con-rod is not a simple compressive strut but has a flailing action that imposes a greater need for rigidity in the plane of its motion than in the plane of the crankshaft, so the tube of the shank would have to be elliptical rather than circular. Scarcely anybody has bothered; but many makers of two-stroke engines, and BMW perhaps alone among the four-strokes until they adopted car-type conrods in 1969, reached a reasonable approximation with a solid shank of elliptical section. This distributes its mass so as to give the preferred orientation of beam stiffness, and it also minimises the aerodynamic drag of a rod moving fast through the air trapped in the crankcase – a form of parasitic loss that has recently been recognised as significant in high-speed engines. Quite apart from this drag, the highly tuned two-stroke cannot afford to have its carefully cultivated flow of fresh charge through the crankcase disturbed by a great paddle of a conrod, which is why the rods of high-performance two-strokes look so improbably sharp and slender. As it happens, the con-rod of a two-stroke has an easier task than its four-stroke equivalent: instead of suffering reversals of load from compression to tension in each complete cycle, it is virtually always in compression – and that is why it is safe to cut away the top of the little-end eye to improve the access of lubricating oil to its bearing.

Nevertheless, the knife-blade rod shank is not ideal, and if the loads imposed on the shank made an H-beam desirable, the web of the H should not lie in the plane of the rod's swing, even though that is how it is almost always made. Charles Lafayette Taylor and Roland Cross demonstrated decades ago, and the author several years ago, that the ribs should be extended generously in that plane and the web should lie between them in the plane of the crankshaft; very recently, some racing rods have been made in this style by Cimelli in Italy and have proved very successful – although much of their merit lies in the excellence of their manufacture, notably the overall shot peening of the surfaces of the forgings from which they are made, inducing a compressive stress in the surface of the steel.

Most con-rods are machined from steel forgings, although a few astute car makers cast them instead. During a long production run, forging dies wear so much that the dimensions and weights of the finished rods vary a lot, making large surplus masses of metal necessary if the danger of an undersized rod is to be avoided. Appropriate amounts may then be ground or milled away, to reduce all rods to equal weight, and it is common to see large projecting bosses of superfluous metal projecting from the big-end cap and the little end to allow for

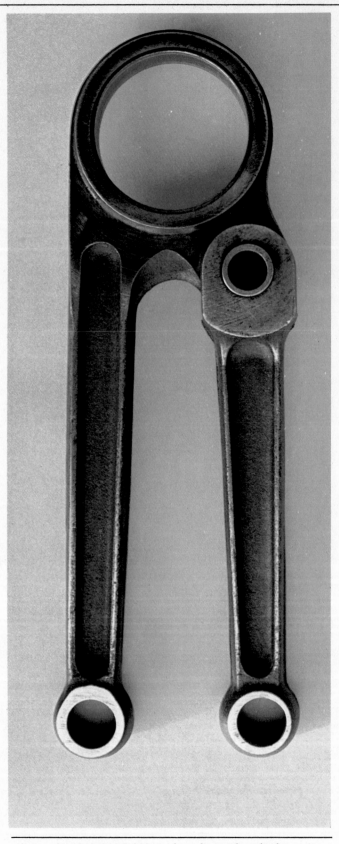

Above: the 1948 EMC 350 used a split-single-cylinder, twin-piston, two-stroke engine. The two cylinders – one for exhaust and inlet and one for mixture transfer, sharing a common combustion chamber – were in a line at right angles to the axis of the crankshaft and parallel to each other, necessitating the use of this articulated, forked con-rod. Similar rods were used in radial and rotary engines.

such balancing operations. A cast rod is naturally more substantial because its metal is less strong, but it is dimensionally more consistent, so the big balancing lugs can be omitted, freeing all the material for useful work. Thus, a cast rod can actually be lighter than a forged one – and lightness is of tremendous importance, affecting engine performance and balance. Many motor cycle engines have successfully employed aluminium-alloy rods, and racing engines built regardless of cost may exploit titanium; in mass produced machines, weight saving is generally pursued in dimensional design rather than in choice of material.

One of the most vital dimensions is the length of the con rod. A short rod is obviously lighter and stiffer than a long one and, by allowing the whole engine to be reduced in height (or width, as in the case of flat twins such as certain racing BMWs), it encourages further savings in material. On the other hand, a long rod promotes smoother running and allows higher engine speeds to be reached for a given level of mechanical stress. This is because of the different amounts of angular swing of long and short rods in engines of identical piston stroke. If the con-rod could be infinitely long, its angular movement would be infinitely small, the motion of the piston up and down the cylinder would be perfectly harmonic (that is, sinusoidal) and there would be no problems of secondary vibration or bearing velocity change to impede the designer. As things are, the con rod must be of finite and practical length: the conventional distance between the centres of the little and big ends is twice the piston stroke, reducing to 1.8 times as the years pass.

This gives a fair compromise between conflicting requirements. Were the rod shorter, the whole engine could be shorter and lighter, and the piston would travel faster on its approach to, and recession from, top dead centre – with advantages in better breathing on the exhaust and inlet strokes, and better conservation of combustion heat during the expansion phase. If the rod were longer, the maximum piston acceleration at a given crankshaft speed would be less, inertia loads on the piston, rings, rod and crankpin would be correspondingly less, secondary vibrational forces would be reduced (because there

would be less difference between the rates of piston acceleration on the upward and downward strokes) and frictional losses between piston and cylinder would be reduced (because of the reduction of conrod angular swing). The combustion process might also benefit from the more nearly constant volume of the combustion space when the piston was in the region of top dead centre. Note that mean piston acceleration is irrelevant, as well as virtually incalculable by direct methods; what matters is the maximum acceleration, which can be derived from the formula:

$$\frac{N^2 S}{2189}\left(1 + \frac{1}{2R}\right) \text{ ft per sec per sec}$$

where N is crankshaft rpm, S is the stroke in inches and R is the ratio of con rod length to stroke. This allows some interesting comparisons to be drawn – for example, between a couple of fairly coeval big twins, the Norton 750 Commando and the BMW R75. The Norton is a long-stroke engine with short rods (R = 1.66), the BMW a short-stroke engine with relatively longer rods (R = 1.85), and both of them generate maximum torque at 5000rpm. In doing so, the BMW's pistons reach peaks of about 40,330 ft per sec per sec and those of the Norton 52,057. It may be easier to think of these accelerations if they are expressed in terms of gravitational acceleration or *g*, in which case the BMW piston reaches 1253*g* and the Norton 1617*g* – in other words, it momentarily weighs 1617 times as much as when it is stationary, and that is how the gudgeon pin feels it, too. The R75 engine is safe up to 7000rpm, at which point the maximum piston acceleration climbs to 2456*g*, but if you run the Commando up to 7000, its piston reaches 3170*g*, which illustrates the importance of minimising the weight not only of the piston but also of the connecting rod itself.   LJKS

Below: as well as the overall dimensions of a con-rod, its cross section is also an important factor in endowing it with the desirable characteristics of strength and lightness. The upper rod is of elliptical section and is from a 1969 BMW; the lower, H-section rod is from a later BMW

The Breaking Point

To ensure efficient running of any engine, it is essential that the spark at the plug, which ignites the fuel/air mixture, occurs at precisely the correct moment, lasts for the right length of time, and has a form compatible with the engine characteristics. Although electronically triggered systems – using photocells or magnetic detectors to initiate the spark – are available, their use is still rare and the simple mechanical contact breaker is the most common means of spark triggering.

Although the system is relatively simple, it demands a great deal of accuracy; a four-cylinder four stroke engine running at 8000rpm requires the contact breaker to open and close 16,000 times in a minute – or over 260 times per second – and this places a great strain on the component. Simple routine maintenance and adjustment of this small but vital part, and its timely replacement when necessary, will keep performance and fuel economy at a peak.

The contact breaker – or points – consists of two adjacent contacts, electrically insulated from each other but joined by a spring. One contact is fixed and the other is pivoted, so that relative movement between the two causes them to act as a switch. The pivoted contact has a heel attached and the heel is kept, by spring pressure, in contact with an engine-driven cam. The fixed contact is connected to earth and the moveable one through the primary winding of the coil to the battery, or other current supply. For a magneto ignition system, the moveable contact is connected to the primary winding of the magneto. As the engine turns, the cam causes the two contacts to move apart, causing a voltage surge as the switching occurs. The surge is damped to some extent by the condenser which is connected between the contacts. The surge travels through the primary circuit and induces a large secondary voltage which is distributed at the correct time to the appropriate spark plug.

So long as the parts are in good condition and the engine revs are not excessive, the system is highly efficient. Unfortunately, deterioration can be rapid. There are three main factors which cause this deterioration, wear of the heel which bears on the cam, loss of tension of the spring and erosion of the actual contacts. The first of these causes the spark to be generated progressively later as the cam takes up the larger gap caused by the wear, the second can allow the points to bounce at high speeds, which completely negates any timing,

and the third reduces the intensity and duration of the spark. Heel wear is of course inevitable, although modern fibre or nylon heels have quite a long life expectancy. Wear is minimised by occasional lubrication, which should be sparing so as not to cover the electrical contacts. Loss of spring tension cannot be avoided and should be borne in mind when deciding when to change the points – a high speed random misfire is a fair indication of points bounce. The points themselves are usually of tungsten or platinum to withstand the enormous heat generated by the rapid sparking but even so they have a tendency to melt on their surfaces and develop a pip on one contact and a corresponding crater in the other. Up to a point, this damage can be repaired by carefully rubbing the faces of the contacts on a stone to grind them flat, taking care to keep the faces parallel. Once the points begin to be eroded in this way, however, their life is very limited as the loss of metal reduces heat conduction.

Other than these routine checks, the most important part of points maintenance is setting the fully opened gap to the correct value. Having gained access to the points – whether by removing a distributor cap or cover, or by aligning an inspection hole in the flywheel – the procedure is simple.

Although some systems have used ring cams, or even face cams and rockers, the most commonly used is the eccentric cam type. Adjustment begins with turning the engine until the points are fully opened by the peak on the cam, the gap can then be measured using a feeler gauge of the thickness specified by the manufacturer for the gap. The screw which secures the base plate – on which the fixed point is mounted – is loosened and the base plate moved to adjust the distance between the points. A slot is usually provided in the base plate in which a screwdriver blade can be inserted and twisted to move the plate. The adjustment is correct when the feeler gauge is just

Left: on twin, or multi-cylinder engines it is common practice to use two contact breakers and an appropriate number of peaks on the actuating cam. This is the system used on the twin-cylinder Honda 125, with two contact breakers and a single peak on the cam. A four-cylinder engine would require a cam with two peaks

Below left: the relative positions of the major components of a cam-actuated contact breaker system. Rotation of the eccentric cam causes the points to open at the right time

Below: a variation of the cam-driven contact breaker is this use of a ring cam which rotates around the points

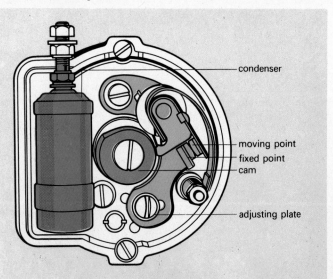

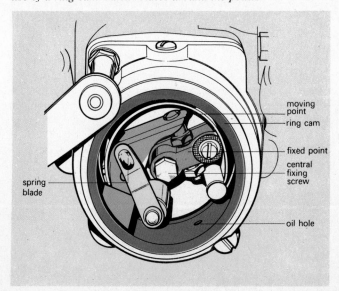

held by the points. The securing screw is tightened and the operation is complete. For any other type of actuation, the adjustment principle is the same; the gap is measured with the points in their fully open position, using a feeler gauge, and moving the normally fixed contact. Dual points should be adjusted individually and the adjustment of one unit should not affect the setting of the other.

With regular attention, the life of the points will be extended, and both performance and fuel economy will benefit – an excellent return for the expenditure of a few minutes work.

Right: the compact electrical system of the BMW R100RS; the contact breaker assembly is at the bottom of the diagram

Below: a one-piece contact breaker set

Bottom: a contact breaker in situ; the cam is also shown

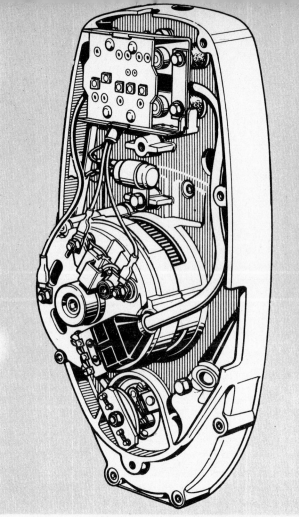

Irrespective of how well a machine performs and how well it is maintained, it can be ruined if it is not comfortable and easy to ride. Compensating for controls which stick or do not work well and forcing yourself into an unnatural position do not only spoil the fun of riding, but they can make it very dangerous. Nine times out of ten, all that is needed is a few drops of oil and ten minutes work with a couple of spanners and a bad machine can literally be transformed.

Throttle

Let us start with the throttle. The brakes are the most important items from a safety point of view but the throttle is the only control which you have to use continuously. If it is stiff, sticks open slightly or if the engine screams away whenever you turn the handlebars, the chances are that it's going to need a new cable. You can change the cable by undoing the screws which clamp the drum on the twistgrip, taking the two halves apart and lifting the nipple from its locating slot. Before you disconnect the cable at the carburettor end, straighten it out and try pulling the inner cable out – it could be that the only problem is a tight turn in the cable, or the cable being trapped by the fork legs or where it passes underneath the petrol tank. Where one cable has to operate several carburettors, the linkage or junction box may be sticking and can be eased off by cleaning up the pivots. If the cable has a kink or a permanent set in it, or if the outer has been chafed and worn through, the best thing is to throw it away.

Cables, like all moving parts, need lubrication. Some machines have nipples fitted to the outer cables so that lubricant can be pumped in using a gun. Otherwise it is a question of persuading light oil to run down inside the cable, a messy and unpredictable affair. The best way to do it is with a cable lubricator, available from most accessory shops, which consists of a small reservoir, with a sealed clamp to hold the outer cable. Oil from the reservoir drains down inside the cable, or there may be a small plunger pump which will speed things up.

While the twistgrip is off, check its action, clean out the drum and repack the sliding parts with a medium grease, using grease between the handlebar and the metal part of the twistgrip. Cable controls will not suffer if you are fairly liberal with grease, because if all the holes are already full of grease, water will not be able to get in. Just wipe off the surplus afterwards so that none gets on to the twistgrip rubber. Check the run of the cable, moving the handlebars from lock to lock to make sure that it cannot develop any tight turns or get trapped when the forks move.

On the assumption that the carburettors are correctly adjusted, the throttle cable adjuster should only be used to take backlash out of the cable itself. Slacken the locknut on the adjuster and turn the adjuster screw out until there is just perceptible movement at the twistgrip before the throttles start to open, then tighten the locknut again.

The throttle action should be smooth and light, no matter what position the handlebars are in and, when you let go of the twistgrip, it should click shut. Many models have a friction screw on the twistgrip – while you are messing about with the throttle it should be backed right off and even in normal use it does not serve any useful purpose.

Brakes

The next item concerns brakes whose controls should also work as smoothly and freely as possible. The same applies to cable operation as for the throttle, while rod linkages should be periodically dismantled, cleaned and assembled with a smear of grease on the pivots. Once again, a blob of grease can prevent water, road dirt or mud from clogging up the pivoting linkage but do not use any lubricant where it could find its way inside the brake drum. Drum brakes have two adjustments, one for the brake and one for the operating mechanism. The handlebar adjuster and the screw-stop on the pedal have nothing to do with the brakes: they simply determine where the lever is when the brake starts to bite and should be used to

Below: there are several products on the market designed to insulate and protect mechanical and electrical components against dampness. A squirt of the liquid silicone inside the vulnerable plug cap is a good idea and the plug leads themselves can be similarly treated

make this suit the size of your hand or foot.

The cable adjuster will be a screw thread in the handlebar lever, either with a lock nut or with a click-stop mechanism. Set it so that the lever has free play until it reaches the most comfortable position for your hand span, with the proviso that this does not allow it to be pulled right back until it is touching the handlebar. If a stoplight switch is operated by the front brake this will also need adjusting afterwards. The pedal stop should be adjusted so that the pedal rests just under your foot or so that you can slide your foot straight across onto it. The brake adjuster should be set so that the brake bites with your foot in the best position for maximum pressure with enough comfort to be able to feel the brake and control it. At 70mph, you are covering more than 100 feet per second and every tenth of a second you waste in reaching for the controls is another ten feet travelled.

Hydraulic brakes are essentially non-adjustable but many have a small screw and locknut which governs the free play before the lever operates the master cylinder. This should be used to set the lever up for the most comfortable operating position, not to take up excessive movement which will probably be due to pad or disc wear or a fault in the hydraulic system.

Clutch

Like the brakes, the clutch has two adjustments, one for the clutch itself and one for the cable. After the clutch is adjusted

Right: brake and clutch cables are usually fitted with knurled adjusters at the lever end, so that any cable slack can be taken up without tools being required

Below: tools are not usually necessary for fitting cables either, the ends being slotted into the levers

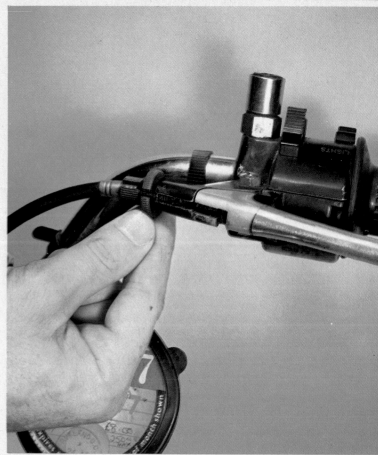

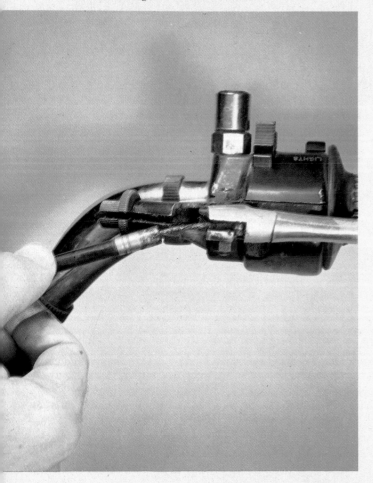

(which is done with the cable slackened right off), the cable adjuster is used to tighten the cable up, leaving 5 or 6mm of free play in the cable. This is to ensure that the cable is not in any tension, which would put a load on the clutch-release mechanism and either cause the clutch to slip or damage the release bearing by making it overheat.

To remove clutch and brake cables, pull in the lever and slowly release it, at the same time pulling the outer cable away from the lever. The outer will come away from the lever and the cable can then be swung forward over the fixed end of the lever and the nipple pushed out of the lever blade. As well as lubricating the cable regularly, inspect it for signs of damage – chafing on the outer cable where it passes the steering head or follows a tight radius and signs of fraying on the exposed part of the inner cable. It is a good idea to carry spare cables, and the best place is alongside the existing one. This way they do not take up any space in the tool compartment, do not get kinked by having them tightly coiled and they are already threaded into place should they be needed. Use PVC tape to hold them to the existing cables and seal the exposed ends with a blob of heavy grease.

Riding position

The next item affords less adjustment on most machines but it is important to make use of as much adjustment as there is. This is the riding position, which is governed by the seat position and its relationship to the footrests and handlebars.

On some machines, the footrest position can be altered slightly, and the handlebar clamps can be slackened to allow the bars to be pivoted an inch or two backwards or forwards. The only alternative is to fit new bars and footrests, which involves making up new pedals and linkages. The object is to make the machine as comfortable as possible, bearing in mind that what feels comfortable at rest need not be so when a 70mph wind is trying to push you off the back of the machine.

Ideally, the rider should be leaning forward enough to balance this force, with hands at shoulder width, elbows slightly bent and wrists at a natural angle to the arms. The footrests should be approximately below the seat, with rather less than a right angle between thigh and calf, so that some weight is taken naturally through the legs and not all of it through the seat. The levers and controls should then be placed so that hands and toes reach them naturally, with the minimum of movement. The gear lever should be moved on its splines, or the linkage adjusted so that you can make upward and downward changes without taking your foot from the footrest. This kind of riding position has been found to give the best comfort and ergonomics in general, but in particular for high-speed cruising. At lower speeds, it is not so important to be leaning forward and in some cases a more upright position with wider handlebars may be better. Off-road riding and use in very heavy traffic or with a pillion passenger are usually better in a more upright position.

Switches

The only other controls on most machines are electrical and, as most current models have complex switches which do not take kindly to being dismantled, prevention is most certainly better than an attempted cure. Water and corrosion are the biggest problem for switches and the best safeguard is one of the water repellant, for which silicon sprays are available. These are intended to insulate electrical parts, so take care not to spray them inside switches, only over the external insulation. Exposed terminals, such as battery connections, can be protected by smearing them with petroleum jelly.

Electrical cables need as much care as control cables where they are exposed to chafing, particularly where the fairly thick, not-too-flexible wiring harness passes between the front forks and the steering head. This can cause two problems. First, chafing and stretching can damage the wiring, causing either a break or a short circuit. Second, the stiffness of the wiring harness can affect the steering, like having an overtightened head bearing.

Instrument cables

There is one other kind of cable used on motor cycles which is worth mentioning. Speedometer and tachometer cables should not be oiled but need a medium grease. If the knurled screw under the instrument head is undone the outer cable will pull away and the inner can be slid out of the instrument and then pulled from the outer. It should be wiped clean and, if it has been damaged or is fraying, replaced (the outer and the inner can usually be bought separately). Smear the inner with grease, leaving the last three inches closest to the instrument clean. This is because the lubricant can work its way up into the instrument, where it will affect its operation. Slide the inner into the outer until it meets resistance, then push gently on it and turn the wheel slowly (for speedometers) or turn the engine on the kick-starter for tachometers. The squared end of the cable will slot into its drive and you will feel the cable turn. Now feed the bare end of the inner into the instrument and make sure it engages by continuing to turn the wheel/engine slowly. Tighten the knurled nut to the instrument head.

This covers the basic controls and their maintenance, but remember that their bad placing leads to fatigue. And a fatigued rider is *not* a safe rider.   VM

Below: throttle cable adjustment is usually allowed for at the carburettor end of the cable, rather than the twist-grip end; the method of adjustment varies, but with the common slide-type throttle, a hexagonal adjuster takes up cable slack after a lock nut has been loosened

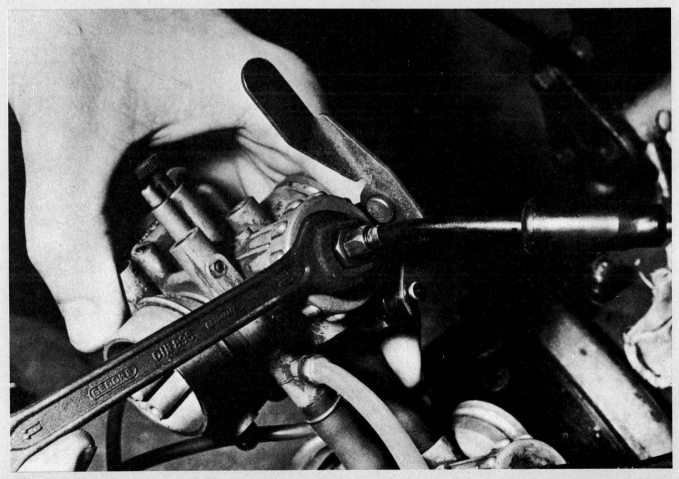

Keeping your Cool

IT SEEMS BEYOND CONTRADICTION that if you introduce cold air and cold fuel into a cold engine you will experience some difficulty in getting and keeping them hot; and the internal-combustion device propelling motor cycles is supposed to be a heat engine. In fact, it works most efficiently when hot, and if all the heat generated within it could be conserved it would be much more efficient and much less fuel-consumptive than anything we have ever known. Alas, the materials available for the construction of a practical engine cannot stand this treatment, and if there were no steps taken to dissipate the heat fed into them, they would (to corrupt Shakespeare) melt, thaw, and resolve themselves into adieu. It is possible to overdo it: P. C. Vincent, the engineer best remembered for his eponymous motor cycles, once built an experimental engine with exceptionally generous cooling provisions, and was rewarded for his trouble with an engine so resolutely cool that it was unable to develop enough heat to warm up the internals. In practice, the engine stopped as soon as the starter was switched off, even with no load applied; the only measurable output was a black and viscid stream of mixed oil and petrol trickling from the exhaust pipes.

Since the waste heat generated by a motor cycle has ultimately to be shed into the air, all motor cycles are ultimately air-cooled; but air is not always the most effective medium for removing heat from some critical region deep within an engine, so water or oil may act as an intermediary. The amount of heat to be shed is considerable: of all the calorific value of the fuel consumed by the engine, only about one third is converted into useful work, the remainder being lost in roughly equal proportions through the exhaust and cooling systems.

The cooling system of a motor cycle includes all the exposed surfaces of the engine from which waste heat is radiated, from the crankcase to the camshaft covers, and if these are polished they cannot get rid of heat very effectively. A matt surface is preferable, and if it be coated with a thin layer of matt black paint it will be better still: only when the coat of paint is thicker than about 0.015in (0.38mm) does the paint act more as a barrier than as a dissipator; best of all is a black anodised finish. In any case, most of the necessary work is done by more efficient heat-exchangers: the cylinders and cylinder heads may be surrounded by water which is then circulated through a radiator where it gives up its heat to the air, or by metal fins which present a large surface area from which heat may escape.

The choice of air or liquid cooling has always been controversial. Air is cheaper, lighter and more readily obtainable than water; but to remove a given quantity of heat demands four times the weight and four thousand times the volume of air as of water. However, air can be collected and rejected, whereas water must be carried on the machine; and the jacketing, conduits, pump and radiator of a water-cooled engine will probably weigh more than the substantial fins of an air-cooled one. On the other hand, the fins force the cylinders of an air-cooled engine to be more widely separated than those that occupy slender water jackets, so the crankshaft and crankcase must be longer and therefore heavier – or longer and yet equally stiff, even in torsion, and therefore *much* heavier. For an engine of many cylinders, this is the most persuasive objection to air

cooling; for a simple horizontally opposed twin it constitutes no objection whatever.

In either case, appreciable power may be expended by any cooling system in pumping the cooling medium around the engine: whether the pump impels water or air hardly matters. Motor cycle designers have always been optimistic about the circulation of air around the fins of air-cooled engines, and have never bothered to provide the close-pitched fins (about 3mm apart), the close-fitting cowling, and the forced-draught fan, that aviation practice long ago established as providing the best results. The fact that the engine may be sitting in the turbulent wake of the front wheel and forks, so that at speed it may be starved of cooling air other than at its natural extremities, seems never to have been a matter of concern; and the same theoretical surprise may be felt over the fact that in motor cycles with liquid-cooled engines the radiator has

Far left: water cooling found many early applications. The location of the radiator on this Scott must also have provided warm leg shields for the rider in wintry conditions

Left: air cooling is still the most common solution for motor cycles but many modifications of the basic idea appear. This AJW Wolfhound engine uses end plates across the fins to duct air and prevent overspill

Below left: modern version of liquid cooling, as used on the Suzuki GT750

cylinder head can make do with what little air is buffeting around at the back. There have been elaborately finned muffs fitted around the exhaust pipes where they emerge from the head, supposedly to assist in cooling the exhaust region, but all they do is to impede the air flow over the fins around the port proper and make the head run hotter, not cooler. If the air-flow can be properly controlled (which ideally requires shrouds around the fins) the best arrangement is to have air flowing from the inlet side to the exhaust side of the head: the air will be warmed by such heat as it picks up from the inlet side, but will still be cool relative to the much higher temperatures around the exhaust ports, so the cooling capacity of the air will be scarcely impaired. Similar rules govern the flow of water through cooling jackets, for if fresh cool liquid be pumped first to the hottest parts of the engine, it will thereafter be too hot to abstract any more heat from the other parts through which it circulates.

The choice of materials is quite important. Early air-cooled engines had cast-iron cylinders and heads, and suffered so gravely from overheating (except for transverse horizontally opposed engines, with cylinders and heads protruding into the air-stream) that it was probably necessity that mothered the invention of the aluminium-alloy cylinder head, cylinder, and piston – although the chronological order of these developments is slightly uncertain. It was at any rate a long time before air-cooled engines could be run as economically as liquid-cooled ones: they had to be run on a rich mixture so that they were partly fuel cooled.

Some of the earliest water-cooled engines had no radiators and no circulatory systems: they relied on the evaporation of the coolant, but this is extremely rare in motor cycle usage, being confined almost entirely to short-spell sprinters. When a closed circuit utilising a radiator was evolved, natural convection currents were trusted to keep the water circulating. The introduction of an engine-driven water pump improved the efficiency of the water-cooled system considerably as well as giving the motor cycle designer more freedom in the location of the radiator, which no longer need be above the engine.

In either kind of system, heat transfer is most efficient when the surface giving up heat to the air is very much hotter than the air – in other words, when the temperature gradient is steep. This has already been mentioned as the reasoning for the reversal of the cylinder head from its conventional orientation, but it has further significance: it makes small closely pitched fins better than large coarse ones on an air-cooled cylinder, and in very hot climates it makes air-cooling better than water.

The effectiveness of a water-cooling system may be improved by raising the temperature of the coolant: the introduction of ethylene glycol, popular today as an anti-freeze, was originally based on its boiling point being very much higher than that of water. It was a troublesome fluid, however, and experimental work showed that by pressurising the cooling system to about 40psi, water could be kept liquid at the same temperature (about 130°C) without boiling. Some glycol could be retained as an anti-freeze agent, but more than 30% is undesirable: water is a better coolant than any other liquid of the same temperature, so superior is its heat transfer ability.

conventionally been located in that same suspect place, with only the radiator of the Honda Gold Wing enjoying the assistance of air deflectors to gather a sufficient flow through the core.

Much more critical is the ease with which the coolant can be brought into contact with the heat at its source. It is a matter of the designer's competence in arranging for water to be guided as near as possible to the spark-plug bosses and exhaust-valve seats of a four-stroke (or the exhaust ports of a two-stroke) to name two of the most important zones, or for their heat to be guided through properly shaped fins to where the air can flow over their surfaces. Here again, motor cycle practice has ignored the lessons of aviation: it is conventional to set air-cooled cylinder heads with their exhaust ports facing forward, it being supposed that they will thus benefit from the full blast of the cooling air stream, whereas the cooler inlet side of the

319

Indeed, the higher the boiling point the better does water compare with any other liquid coolant in this respect, so that adding even a small amount of water to glycol makes it a lot better. By the time the proportions reach 70% water to 30% glycol, heat transfer is virtually as good as with plain water, and the resistance of the mixture to freezing or the dangerous slushing process that precedes it is adequate outside regions suffering winters of arctic severity.

Most modern water-cooled machines have their systems pressurised, a spring-loaded filler-cap or valve preventing the blowing off of steam or heat-expanded water until the pressure within the system has risen to 7 or even 14psi. The higher the pressure, the higher the temperature at which water boils, and at 7psi above atmospheric the boiling point of water is postponed from 100 to 112°C. The greater efficiency of these high-pressure systems allows the radiator to be made smaller, lighter and cheaper. There is a slight incidental danger: at pressures above 4psi, the old-fashioned fail-safe bellows-type thermostat valve may be forced to close, whereas the modern wax-filled type is not affected by pressure but is not a fail-safe component, for if it does not work properly it will not open when it should.

The presence of the thermostat valve is explained by the need for the liquid-cooled engine to be brought up to its normal working temperature as quickly as possible, for an engine is most inefficient when running cooler than necessary. The bulk of the cooling water is therefore isolated from the engine by this valve, allowing the relatively small amount in the engine's water jackets to be heated quickly. When working temperature is reached, the valve opens and normal circulation begins.

The reason for having a large mass of water in the total system is that it constitutes a valuable safety barrier against overheating when the engine is subjected to brief spells of very arduous duty. The water can accept a lot of surplus heat that can thereafter be shed steadily over a fairly long period; it is also much easier to design an engine in which the cooling water can be guided very close to hot-spots such as exhaust ports and sparking plug bosses, and this is almost essential for a durable highly supercharged engine, as it has proved for highly tuned racing two-strokes. Air-cooling can muster neither of these advantages: the air cannot be brought so close to these sources of intense heat, which therefore have to be content to divine the cooling medium at a distance, and there is no heat-buffer in reserve. In such conditions, the air-cooled engine puts more heat into its lubricating oil (which is in any case the immediate transfer medium for removing heat from pistons, piston rings and bearings), so it is usual for an air-cooled engine to require a heat-exchanger (oil-cooler) for its oil if it be a high performance machine – and this cooler, although smaller and lighter than a water radiator, is unlikely to be any cheaper.

These radiators always used to be made of copper, a material having exceptionally good thermal conductivity. Aluminium has recently come into limited use instead for, although its conductivity is slightly inferior, it is much lighter. Either metal may suffer or cause galvanic corrosion, according to the other materials present in the cooling system, and it is common nowadays for carefully formulated corrosion inhibitors to be added to the water or to the anti-freeze, according to the metals involved. Thus, an aluminium and iron engine may need a different additive from one with an all-aluminium construction. Some of the latest anti-freeze fluids on the market have universal inhibitors added to make them suitable for engines with any combination of materials in their water circuitry, but great care should be taken to ensure that the anti-freeze agent is ethylene glycol: some cheap anti-freezes contain a large admixture of alcohol and deteriorate rapidly but unmeasurably due to loss by evaporation. Evaporative cooling was once popular among theoreticians; evaporative freezing has no attractions at all. LJKS

Below: this cutaway diagram shows the flow of coolant through the flat-four engine and cooling system of the 1977 Honda GL1000 Goldwing. Although fairly rare in a road bike, water cooling is common on large racers

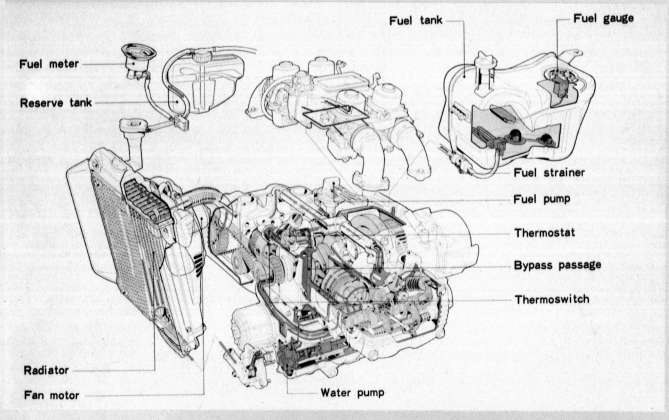

Round the Bend

IN CORNERING TERMS, a single-track vehicle is an entirely different proposition from a multi-track vehicle such as a car: the former must be banked over in the direction of turn to go round at all, whereas the latter tends to lean *away* from the corner under centrifugal force.

There are three stages in negotiating a corner on a two wheeler. The first is a 'transient state' and consists of shifting the plane of the machine and rider from the vertical to the inclination necessary for rounding the corner. Next, we have the 'steady state' where the motor cycle is in equilibrium, cornering at a constant angle of bank and theoretically capable of continuing to do so, on a maintained radius, until it runs out of fuel.

A good rider delights in this smooth progression round a corner or bend, but an inexperienced or clumsy one may take several bites at the cherry, going round in a series of minor adjustments to the line and the angle of bank. Also, of course, road surfaces are rarely dead smooth: a bump can deflect the steering and so necessitate correction by the rider in order to hold the chosen path.

Correction can also be compelled by the fact that many corners do not have a constant radius. Where the whole of the bend is in view, the rider may be able to choose a line that gives him a circular arc of progress once he has the adopted cornering attitude. However, most of us have encountered the blind bend that tightens-up part-way round, and for this the bike must of course be leaned farther over.

The final stage of the cornering sequence is the reverse of the first – namely the restoration of the machine from the banked condition to the vertical, so that it can continue stably in a straight line.

As in the case of low-speed balancing, most riders very soon master the basic cornering technique which then becomes second nature in normal circumstances. The interesting thing here is that the big majority acquire this proficiency automatically and cannot say exactly what they do to enter or leave a corner.

Simple dynamics

Because the whole two-wheeler cornering procedure is founded on the machine having to be in a banked condition, it is logical to have a closer look at the 'steady state' before we consider the entry and exit. For our purposes here we need to take account of only two forces that act on the machine – its weight and the centrifugal force arising from its curved path.

By definition, both these forces act through the centre of gravity of the machine/rider combination, the weight vertically downward and the centrifugal force horizontally outward. For equilibrium – that is, for no tendency to increase or decrease the angle of bank – the resultant of these forces must pass through the ground line joining the contact centres of the front and rear tyres.

In practice, that resultant has to be divided between the two tyres, proportionally to the front/rear weight distribution. At the contact patches of the tyres, the part-resultants are reacted by the road, the reactions being equal and opposite to the imposed forces. Each reaction can be resolved into an upward component opposing the weight and a horizontal inward one opposing the centrifugal force.

Net yet explained is why the machine automatically follows a curved path when it is in the banked condition, instead of merely falling over. The steering head of a motor cycle is inclined backward from the vertical, and its axis meets the road several inches ahead of the perpendicular through the front-wheel spindle. This combination of head angle and 'trail' is called the steering geometry. When the bike is in the banked state, the steering geometry gives rise to forces which cause the wheel to be turned in the direction of lean. The greater the angle of bank, the more the wheel turns inward to compensate.

Below: cornering this production Triumph Trident is much harder than cornering a purpose-built racer as the centre of gravity is higher and the bike much heavier. However, to get the machine to bank at a greater angle, and therefore corner quicker, side and centre stands are removed from underneath

centrifugal force
centre of gravity of machine and rider
resultant force
weight
angle of bank
tyre contact wire

Above: cornering limits for any vehicle are governed by the laws of dynamics; for a single-track vehicle an essential element is the act of banking through the corner. When cornering the forces acting are the machine's weight, vertically, and centrifugal force acting towards the centre of the curve. The correct banking angle causes the resultant of these forces to pass through the tyre contact line

Because the centrifugal force increases as the square of the angular velocity (that round the centre of rotation), the angle of bank also has to increase rapidly as the rate of turn goes up. One of the diagrams illustrates this by demonstrating the effect of doubling the angular velocity, *ie*, quadrupling the centrifugal force. In the first case, my assumed values result in an angle of bank of only 14° from the vertical, but in the second the angle is no less than 45°!

The next thing to be made clear is that cornering cannot take place at all in the absence of grip between tyres and road to resist the centrifugal force. This fact will be abundantly clear to anyone who has chanced upon a patch of ice or oil in the middle of a corner – the subsequent progress is sideways! Grip has already been discussed under Braking, and it is quantified by what is called the 'coefficient of friction'. This coefficient can vary over quite a wide range according to the nature of the road surface: it can be as low as about 0.1 on wet ice and maybe as high as 1.2 where modern racing tyres are running on good dry tarmac.

The coefficient of friction is the maximum horizontal force that can be developed without sliding, divided by the vertical force applied – the weight of the machine and rider in this context. If the coefficient is known, the maximum angle of bank without lateral sliding can readily be determined, since the coefficient is the tangent (a trigonometrical ratio) of that angle. Putting in some values, a coefficient of 0.6 – typical for a wet road – means a limiting angle of 31° from the vertical, whereas with the previously mentioned 1.2 the angle could be as much as 50° from the vertical, or more than 'half-way over', before adhesion is lost.

Leaning and sliding

For any particular angle of bank of the machine/rider combination, the inclination of the machine itself can be varied quite considerably by the rider altering his attitude or position.

The individual centres of gravity are shifted thereby, but their combined one does not (see illustration). One option is for the rider to lean away from the corner, so the bike has to be banked farther; alternatively, he can lean into the corner or move his weight in that direction, thus reducing the inclination of the machine.

The leaning-out technique can be helpful in the rare case of a motor cycle with steering geometry that does not cause the front wheel to turn-in quite enough on its own. Then, the extra amount of bank increases the turn-in, thus making it unnecessary for the rider to apply a steering torque to the handlebar to keep on line. However, the additional lean of the bike makes 'grounding' of the exhaust system or a footrest more likely in hard cornering, and it can also bring the contact area of the tyres too far round onto the shoulder.

Conversely, the leaning-in or weight-in method could be used if one had a machine on which the front wheel tended to turn-in too much – also very rare these days. It is widely employed by racers, however, to minimise unwanted contact with the road and to keep the tyres as upright as possible. Many racing men combine a weight-shift with sticking-out the inside knee in the belief that, at speed, the additional aerodynamic drag on that side of the bike helps it round the corner. Aerodynamicists are in general sceptical of the effectiveness of this ploy, but few of them ride racing motor cycles!

The available tyre grip for cornering is greatest when the wheel concerned is being neither accelerated under power nor braked. This is because some longitudinal grip is required for the acceleration or braking, and consequently less remains in the lateral direction.

If a motor cycle is being cornered 'on the limit' and the rider opens the throttle (assuming he is not already flat-out), the rear wheel will lose adhesion – to an extent depending on the amount of additional torque applied to it – and will therefore slide outward under the centrifugal force. The same will

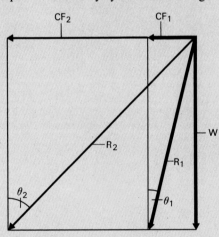

Above: centrifugal force (CF$_x$) varies with the square of angular velocity, so CF$_2$=4CF^1 and the angle of bank, θ, increases dramatically from θ$_1$=14° to θ$_2$=45°

Right and far right: the resultant of the weight and centrifugal forces must act through the combined centre of gravity of the rider and machine. The true banking angle is thus the angle of a line passing through the combined centre of gravity and the tyre contact line. Relative movement between rider and machine can be used to vary the actual angle of the machine

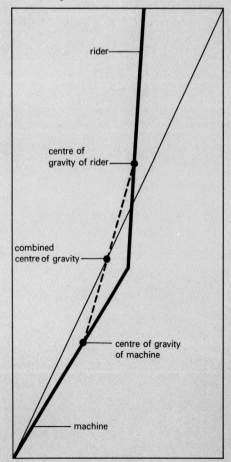

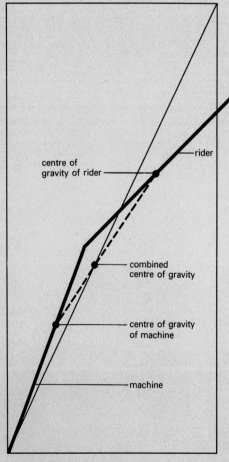

happen if the rear brake is applied, while operation of the front brake will of course cause the front wheel to slide. Hence, the rider should normally complete his braking before getting right into the corner and should not turn on the power until he is coming out of it. There are occasions, though, when a *controlled* amount of power-sliding can be used to help the back-end round. The extreme case here is the dirt-track 'broad-siding' technique in which the machine is held under power at a considerable angle to the direction of travel.

Entering and leaving the corner

It is quite widely believed that a rider banks his machine into a turn by pressing down on the appropriate footrest and/or using his knees on the petrol tank to 'nudge' the bike over. Some banking by these means is certainly possible with an ordinary motor cycle, but what of the scooter on which one sits with the feet quite close together (where they can exert little lateral leverage) and with no tank between the knees? Since we have all seen scooters being cranked over and picked up again very briskly, there must be more to it than feet and knees. The 'magic ingredient' is in fact the handlebar, and what happens is really an extension of the balancing sequence.

Let us assume that the rider wishes to go round a left-hand bend. First he steers to the *right* by pulling on the right grip and pushing on the left. The resulting angular velocity produces a centrifugal force acting to the left through the centre of gravity. This force causes the machine to roll to the left, so the front-wheel spindle is tilted laterally from the horizontal. When any flywheel is so treated it tries to precess – that is, the axis wants to tilt in a direction at right angles to the imposed movement. Hence, the front wheel receives a precessional torque to the left.

The rider resists the precession initially as the machine continues to roll to the left, but as it approaches the desired angle of bank he eases his torque on the handlebar. So, the front wheel is turned-in by the precessional torque, which is aided now by the steering geometry; the turning-in kills the original leftward centrifugal force and hence the roll. As the machine immediately starts turning left, the necessary rightward centrifugal force is generated to counter the toppling-over effect of

the weight, and the bike is set-up for the corner.

Previously I mentioned the possibility of a rider encountering a bend that tightens part-way round. To cope with this, he has to use the same technique again: he applies right-hand torque briefly to the handlebar to *reduce* his rate of turn and therefore the centrifugal force. Consequently, the weight takes effect to pull the machine farther from the vertical. The rider then releases the handlebar torque and equilibrium is restored at the greater angle of bank, but with a higher angular velocity and hence more centrifugal force.

The process is reversed for the return to the vertical. A left-handed torque on the handlebar is used to increase the angular velocity and therefore the centrifugal force. This greater force overcomes the effect of the weight, causing the machine to roll to the right. As it approaches the upright attitude, the rider eases his torque and so the wheel straightens-up and the centrifugal force dies away. AB

Right: the rider of this BMW R100RS should find cornering a pleasure since the bike, big though it is, is beautifully balanced

FROM RUSSIA WITH LOVE

Soviet motor cycles are becoming more and more of a common sight, and Cossacks produce a comprehensive line of machines, from 125cc though to 650cc.

Whereas a motor cycle marque name, almost without exception, is that of the actual constructor, the Cossack name more truly relates to the country of origin – the USSR. The reason for this is the fact that the Soviet motor cycle industry is set up in quite a different way from the industries of the West. While the western factories each organise their own sales arrangements, the Soviet system is quite unusual. One organisation, namely 'Vsesouznoje Objedinenije Avtoexport', is responsible for the exportation of all Soviet motor cycles, mopeds and motor scooters. In addition, it also handles cars, trucks, buses, tractors and so on, and has over one hundred and twenty-five major factories producing them. The motor cycle industry is comprised of a relatively small group of plants, each generally producing one type of motor cycle. One reason why Soviet motor cycles are gaining in popularity is their highly competitive prices; the fact that complete factories make just one machine is an important factor in this. Likewise, there is not any desperate drive to produce more and different new models every year. Thus, once a factory is tooled up, it can concentrate on improving its output without being lumbered with design changes at regular intervals.

One national organisation, the CKEB in Moscow, is responsible for all motor cycle design, and feeds all the factories with any ideas that its engineers develop. The design of Cossack–Soviet motor cycles, as already inferred, do not change very frequently. Thus the factories can produce large numbers of one type machines; in fact, the Soviet Union is now the second largest motor cycle producer in the world; in 1975, for instance, it produced 1.65 million machines. Considering the small range of machines, compared with the scores from the number one producer Japan, this is no small achievement.

The Soviet motor cycle industry came into being, it seems, in the late 1920s and early 1930s. Machines built in those early days were of many different types, ranging from two-stroke twins and singles to transverse twins and 'V' twins

of capacities up to 1200cc.

However, very little was seen of them until long after World War II, that is to say, outside the Soviet Union itself. In fact, only as recently as 1958, when the current range was exhibited at the World Fair in Brussels, were enthusiasts able to see what was being produced in the East.

The range shown did not include all the bikes produced, but it was representative of the normal road-going machines that were then being produced in quantity. Smallest in the lineup was the K-58, a 125cc single-cylinder two-stroke with a three-speed gearbox. Very much the Soviet equivalent of the popular BSA Bantam of the time, it had a lowly 6.5 to 1 compression ratio, and a claimed output of 56bhp. Wheels were interchangeable, and it had telescopic forks and swinging-arm rear suspension; tyres were small section, being 2.50m × 19in. Ideal for the commuter, this machine was not an ideal mount for two people, and for this the Russians offered the K175. Again a single-cylinder two-stroke, it was a twin-port device, and produced just three more bhp than the 125cc. Designed more as a touring machine than the 125, it was however more luxurious in appearance. The frame centre section was fully enclosed, as was the chain, and the carburettor was enclosed to give the engine unit a very stylish streamlined appearance. Moving up the capacity scale, the 350cc class was represented by the 350cc Jupiter, a two stroke twin, apparently well built and

well up-to-date with regard to design and general styling. Output of this motor was 18bhp, and the clutch was of the automatic disengaging type. Its gearbox contained four gears, and the motor cycle had a top speed of 68.7mph.

Changing the range from two-stroke to four, a 500cc transverse twin was presented. Featuring swinging-arm rear suspension, short leading link forks and shaft drive, it was a machine that attracted a great deal of attention; its designation was M-53. Its ohv twin engine developed 28bhp at 5600rpm, and was a reasonable looking machine, although on the heavy side at 185 kilos.

Having 'broken the ice' as it were, Soviet motor cycles, not yet thought of as 'Cossacks', started to become more common in the West, although they were not destined to come to Britain for many years. In the Soviet Union itself, there was already a healthy interest in motor cycle sport, and a whole range of machines was constructed for it. In fact, in 1958, six competition models were listed, every one a two-stroke, although the big transverse twins, soon appearing as 650 and 750cc models, were active in sidecar competition.

The majority of the special competition models were for off-road sport, which Soviet riders favoured, and were

Below: this is a typical Russian outfit of the early 1960s, the M62 Ypan; it is a 650cc transverse twin producing 28bhp and enabling the outfit to reach 59mph

Below: the old 750cc side-valve, transverse twin, the K-750. This 1965 version had short leading link forks, and produced 2bhp less than the 650cc M-62. Both machines were virtually identical in appearance, but the older model's top speed was 56.2mph

JAMES LEECH

primarily in 125 and 350cc categories. Motor cycles made outside of the USSR were still very scarce, so the sport was almost one marque competition. The most potent of the 125cc models (they all had cylinders of 52mm × 58mm) for off-the-road produced only 6.5bhp at 5000 to 5200rpm. Gearboxes were three-speed units, and the machines were claimed to top 50mph. Their exhaust systems were downswept, and telescopic forks and swinging-arm rear suspensions were standard. The larger models, utilis-ing 346cc single-cylinder engines (of different pattern to those by this time powering a 350cc roadster to complement the twin) had four gears and upswept twin exhaust systems and they produced 16bhp.

In 1961, some improved versions of these machines did turn up in Britain in a large team sent over for the ISDT in Wales. These were in 173, 246, 346, and 352cc sizes, and designated K175, IZH240, IZH60, and IZH500. Very rugged motor cycles, they were quite a contrast to the more usual ISDT mach-ines of the time.

Road racing was also supported in the Soviet Union, and a couple of 'over-the-counter-racers' were produced in the late 1950s. Yet again, two-stroke singles of 125 and 350cc capacities, they had rigid frames and outputs of 7.5 and 18bhp, respectively.

In the latter 1950s and early 1960s, the sidecar in the West almost became extinct, while in the East quite the opposite was occurring. The big trans-verse twins were ideal sidecar haulers, and the Russians took full advantage. Complete sidecar outfits were and still are being produced in tremendous quan-tities, making the Soviet Union the top world producer in this category.

Meanwhile, the roadster range of two-strokes was continued, the K-175 being improved in 1965 and dubbed the Kov-rovets. The Ural, as the flat twin had been named, was up-dated and called the M-63; the 750cc was simply called the K-750.

The M-63 was improved, and the motor's compression was raised and output increased to 30bhp at 4800 to 5200rpm, but the major changes were in the cycle department.

The frame was brand new, and, of course, incorporating swinging-arm rear suspension. When supplied with a side-car, a spare wheel was also included; the new model also had interchangeable

wheels, a feature very much favoured by the Soviet manufacturers.

The latter part of 1967 saw the introduction of a new model named Voskhod, a 175cc two-stroke single of attractive style, and the ideal commuter machine. In fact, it was supplied complete with legshields, windshield, carrier and a top speed of 56mph. The Voskhod has proven to be a great success ever since for the Russians, and even in 1977 sells well in many countries. Come 1968 and a fresh 125cc lightweight came on to the scene, the M105. Like the larger two-strokes, this one now had partial rear enclosure and a fully enclosed rear chain.

The 350cc single-cylinder Planeta, and the 350cc twin Jupiter were redesigned for 1972, the latter supplied if required with a stylish sidecar. Outputs of these machines were 18 and 25bhp respectively, and marked a new step forward in Soviet motor cycle design. Soon to follow was the Planeta Sport model.

Exports were growing at this time, and the range was brought into Britain in limited numbers. In spite of the intense competition from other countries, especially Japan, they found favour. The year 1974 saw a change of importer in Britain, and a new upsurge in sales. This was the time when the brand name Cossack was introduced, the old marques being retained as model names.

The smallest model imported in 1977 is the 125cc Minsk, which is a more 'sporty' looking model than the M105 it supercedes. With 9.5bhp on tap, it offers, especially for the younger rider, an economical means of transport.

The Voskhod 175 continues to be a popular model, and is surprisingly close in design to the original model of 1967.

The 'touring' Planeta is no longer brought into Britain, but the sport version is, and, with an output of 32bhp, a top speed of nearly 88mph is claimed. No rear chain enclosure or body styling here, but then it is only a sports model. Those who want a touring 350, however, can have one in the form of the Jupiter twin, developed from the new one introduced in 1972.

Finally, top of the range are a pair of the famous 650cc transverse four-stroke twins, the Ural, and the more sporty Dnieper. Both engines have the same bore and stroke (78mm × 68mm) and produce the same power, 35bhp at 5200rpm. However, the Dnieper has full-width brakes and other detail modifications to make it the best Cossack.　DJ

Left: this model is little, graceful and no doubt fun to ride with. By contrast, the bike, a Denieper MT9 solo is rugged, reliable and equally powerful

Far left: the 350cc ISDT machine of 1961, known as the IZH60 or the Isch

Cossack Dnieper MT-9

Just looking at a 650cc Cossack Dnieper combination, one thinks of a vintage BMW outfit. That is hardly surprising as the Russian machine is indeed based on an early German bike.

Although this means that the bike is extremely rugged and reliable, it also means that the Cossack is out as far as sporting motor cycling is concerned.

In fairness, though, the Russian machine is intended as a cheap-to-run machine for up to three people. The performance is adequate, the economy is outstanding and the maintenance bills should be too few to mention.

The basis of the outfit is a flat-twin pushrod engine of 649cc which produces a very leisurely 32bhp. With a sidecar (which is mounted on the right, incidentally), the top speed is 63mph while fuel consumption works out at a very respectable 55mpg: the performance may not be what is expected of a 650 but then neither is the economy, which is a good thing for those who want cheap touring.

Like all combinations, the Cossack needs a whole new riding technique. The steering is naturally heavy at all speeds, while handling is fairly neutral in towns. However, when riding hard, one has to remember two important things: one has to *decelerate* around left-hand corners and *accelerate* around right handers. This is for the left-hand-drive outfits. Naturally, the opposite technique is required for machines with the British sidecar arrangement.

What happens if these techniques are not observed is quite simple: the bike will tend to travel straight on in a situation of what 'on four wheelers' call understeer.

The finish of the Cossack is like most wheeled machines from behind the iron curtain in that it is rugged with very few frills. For example, the riders seat is a single rubber saddle, while the pillion passenger sits on a similar seat perched on the rear mudguard. The sidecar passenger, however, is altogether better catered for and can even listen to the optional stereo!

Once the spare wheel is strapped onto the back of the outfit, there is a distinct lack of luggage space, but that should be no worry for there is a two-wheeled trailer which can be purchased and fitted onto the back of the whole. Or, if one prefers, a trailer with a fold-out tent can be ordered. Does that make the 650cc Dnieper Combination the first ride-on sleep-in motor cycle for the whole family? If so, it is surprising how cheaply it can be bought.

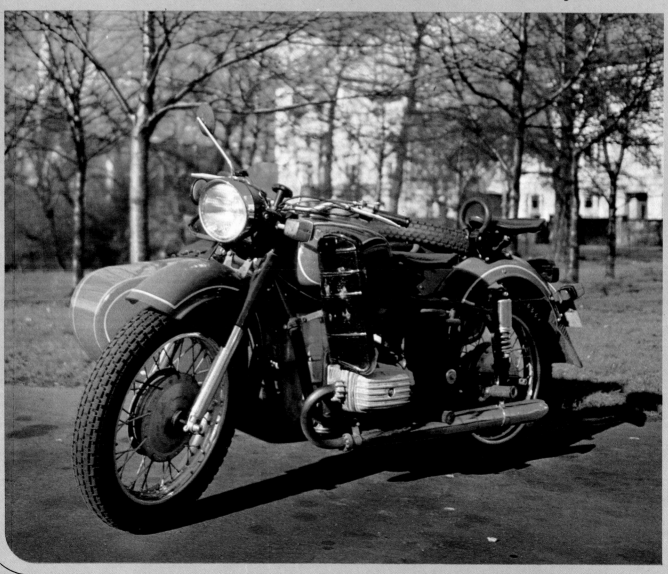

Engine
Air-cooled flat-twin four-stroke. 78mm (3.07in) × 68mm (2.68in) stroke = 649.9cc. Maximum power (DIN) 35bhp at 5200rpm. Aluminium-alloy cylinder barrels and heads. Compression ratio 7:1. 2 main bearings; 2 valves per cylinder operated via pushrods and rockers by a single central camshaft. Twin K/3016 carburettors.

Transmission
Single dry-plate clutch and four speed gearbox; sidecar outfit has reverse gear. Left-foot change; ratio: 1st 2.77, 2nd 1.76, 3rd 1.30, 4th 1.00:1. Shaft and hypoid bevel final drive to rear wheel, ratio 6:1.

Suspension
Front, telescopic forks with coil springs and hydraulic dampers. Rear, swinging arm with double dampers.

Brakes
Drum brakes front and rear.

Wheels and tyres
3.75in × 19in all round, including sidecar and spare.

Weight
464lb (210kg) solo; 696lb (315kg).

Tank capacity
4.1 gallons (18.86 litres), 91 octane fuel.

Seating
Individual saddles for rider and passenger; dual seat optional. Sidecar seats one adult comfortably.

Performance
Maximum speed, 78.1mph solo; 62.5mph combination. Fuel consumption 55mpg.

*Above: a purposeful Cotton trials bike
of 1976, fitted with a 250cc DMW
engine*

*Below left: Peter Inchley rides a 250cc
Cotton Conquest during the 1965 500
Mile Race at Castle Coombe, Witlshire*

Present-day motor cyclists might
wonder what gave the Gloucester-
based Cotton factory such an un-
doubted advantage in the years between
the wars. After all, Cotton machines used
the same proprietary engines – Blackburne, JAP, Villiers, Rudge Python and
even the occasional Bradshaw – as did
most other small manufacturers. How
did they come to win races all over the
country adding a number of world speed
records for good measure?

The answer lay in a rather unconventional frame; light, yet scientifically triangulated in two planes, affording a low
centre of gravity and a low seating position. In a period when the majority of
makers stuck to a frame that was still, in
essence, a basic bicycle diamond shape,
the Cotton was the bike that handled
best. It may have been no quicker than
its rivals in a straight line, but the frac-
tions of a second gained by superior
handling qualities all mounted up. This
was the secret of its success.

Frank Willoughby Cotton, better
known as Bill Cotton, was a native of the
Ledbury area of Herefordshire and came
from farming stock. However, he himself elected to study law, and it was in his
student years that he began to compete
in local trials and hill-climbs, mainly on
an open-frame Scott.

Now, Alfred Scott was an engineering
genius who scorned accepted theories and
struck out along a path of his own. Even
in the 1912–13 period, the Scott frame
displayed a measure of triangulation, and
it could well have been this that inspired
Bill Cotton to devise a triangulated
frame of his own. The result did not look
much like the Scott frame, but it followed
the same broad path of lightness and
rigidity.

From the steering head, four straight
tubes, two at each side, ran direct to the
rear fork ends. There were widely spaced
chain stays and torque tubes, and a pair
of splayed front down tubes to hold the
engine and gearbox firmly in place, and
so check any tendency to flex under
power.

Through his own competition riding
around the Midlands, Bill had come to
know the Butterfield brothers, who ran
the Levis works, and it was to them that
he now turned. A couple of frames of
Cotton design were constructed by
Levis, and one frame was used to house
something of a 'rogue' engine – an
experimental 350cc two-stroke Levis
twin, with such a vicious couple that a
normal frame was unsuitable. Several
years later, this same engine was fitted
into a conventional frame by the late Bob
Burgess; it broke the front down tube –
twice!

Very impressed with the frame, the

It's a Frame up

The success of Cotton bikes is directly related to the sophisticated frame, originally developed in 1913, and soon to appear again on the road-racing scene.

Levis people suggested that they should use it for their own machines, paying Bill Cotton a royalty on each example, but by this time World War 1 had begun, and it was becoming evident that production would have to wait until the return of peace, in any case. Bill, wisely, had applied for a patent, and this was duly granted to him as Patent No. 17434/1914. For the next year or two, he devoted himself to developing his idea to production readiness, but in truth he was in something of a quandary.

Should he continue his law studies, meanwhile drawing a steady income in royalties from the Levis factory? Or should he abandon his career and take the big gamble of becoming a manufacturer in his own right?

He chose the second course and, late in 1918, he acquired a small building at 11a Bristol Road, Gloucester, which is still a motor cycle shop to this day, although, its connection with Cotton was severed long ago. Dismissing any thought of a lash-up frame jig, he ordered a comparatively expensive jig with a cast-steel base. That, thought Cotton, should last a long time – and how right he was, because that original cast-steel jig, together with another ordered during the boom years of the mid-1920s, still serves for the Cottons of 1977; both have been

modified over the years, of course, but under the later superstructure, the original triangulated-frame brackets survive.

Announced in the autumn of 1919, the first production Cotton was a modest little model, powered by a 269cc Villiers two-stroke engine with chain drive to a forward-mounted magneto. It had Druid side-spring front forks (Saxon forks, with a single horizontal spring operated through bell-crank levers, were available as an alternative), a two-speed gearbox and belt final drive. In Cotton's first advertisements, the machine is shown with fashionable light-alloy wheel discs clipped to the spokes, but these were optional extras, not included in the list price.

It is questionable how a disc-wheel lightweight would have performed in a crosswind!

For that opening season, sales were low, but things began to perk up when a 350cc side-valve model was added for 1922. The engine was a Blackburne, quite sporty for the time, and when coupled to a three-speed Burman gearbox, gave the Cotton a nippy enough performance.

All the same, in sporting circles the side-valve was already yielding ground to the overhead-valve engine, and when Blackburnes announced that they, too, would market a 350cc of this type, Bill Cotton jumped at the chance. He had no false modesty where his straight-tube

Below: this Cotton Sprint special was built in 1930 and was fitted with a 500cc ohv Blackburne engine

frame was concerned, and Cotton literature of the time emphasised that this was 'the only frame wherein all important connections between steering head and rear spindle are triangulated both vertically and laterally . . . every set of tubes is straight and subjected only to compression and tension . . . it is practically impossible to destroy the alignment of either wheel, even under great stress.'

However, the public had to be convinced of its sterling qualities, and the best way of achieving such an aim was to put up a good showing in some spectacular event – such as the Isle of Man TT. So Bill Cotton entered three machines for the 1922 Junior TT.

This is where fate took a hand, because from out of the blue, Bill Cotton received a letter, ostensibly from the Dublin agent for Harley-Davidson, extolling the virtues of a young Irish rider by the name of Stanley Woods. In fact, Stanley had dictated the letter himself. Son of the Mackintosh Toffee representative for Ireland, he was 18 years old, and had a pal who rode a Harley-Davidson and who, by exercising the imagination to an almost alarming degree, could be described as a motor cycle agent.

In any case, the Irish blarney paid off, and Stanley found himself teamed with Cotton's foreman, later works manager, Fred Morgan, and a Lancashire sand-racing specialist named Harry F. Brockbank. Stanley, plus pal, plus Harley-Davidson, sailed early for the Isle of Man to ensure getting in as much practice as possible; and promptly set off in the wrong direction of the course.

The tipsters of the weekly motor cycling press didn't rate the Cotton entries very highly, but when the Junior TT got under way, folk began to sit up. Here was Woods, the unknown youngster on an unknown bike from the wilds of the West Country, lying an incredible fourth on the first lap! Nor was that the whole story, because as Stanley pushed away from the line he dropped his spare sparking plus, and had actually run back to pick it up before restarting.

Woods was due to refuel at the end of the second lap, and now came near-disaster. At this time, the 'stop engines' rule had not been thought of, and in the current fashion Stanley kept the engine running while fresh petrol was tipped into the Cotton's tank. Suddenly, surplus fuel ran down the tank sides and on to the sparking plug. Stanley's leathers caught fire and, dropping the bike, he dashed across the road to where the attendant fireman had his extinguisher at the ready.

Notwithstanding such a shock to his system, Woods grabbed the bike and got back into the race, working up to sixth place – but soon he was facing more trouble, this time the lack of a rear brake. The blaze had caused the oil compart-

ment of the tank to leak at a seam, and oil, streaming back, was soaking the brake. It was often a matter of footing to get round the corners, but to cheers almost as loud as those reserved for the winner, Woods came home fifth, with the other pair following in 11th and 15th places.

'Watch Woods!', noted *Motor Cycle's* famous columnist, Ixion, and his prediction was amply justified the following year. For his 1923 Junior TT team, Bill Cotton again pinned his faith on Woods, Morgan and Brockbank. 'The Cottons,' wrote *Motor Cycle*, 'are all rare goers, and save valuable seconds on the corners.' They certainly did, thanks to the wonderful straight-tube frame, and Stanley Woods, at only 19 years old, scored the first of his ten TT victories by winning at record speed, even though he had again run out of brakes, and had clouted a wall at Ramsey in consequence.

Now the Cotton began to make itself felt in other fields, too. Blackburne development engineer, Paddy Johnston, won the 250cc class of the Brooklands 200-mile race, and went on to finish second in the French Grand Prix. Woods moved on to pastures new, but Johnston was brought into the TT team in his place. In the newly-introduced 175cc Ultra-Lightweight TT, using tall and thin Blackburne engines which had to be canted to fit them into the frames, Cottons were second, third and fifth in 1924. Other places were gained in the 250cc TT, in the Ulster Grand Prix, and at Brooklands.

With the Cotton's fast-growing reputation, sales doubled and redoubled. The little shop in Bristol Road had soon been outgrown, but Bill Cotton had been able to secure the lease of a factory in Quay Street, Gloucester, at the rear of the famous cathedral. Originally, the

Above: Pat Onions, second from the left, with John Draper, Mike Smith, Fluff Brown, Fred Smith and Lionel Wyre and their Cotton machines

Below: Scott Farweather takes to the air in the 1932 Lightweight TT on his Cotton

Above: the Blackburne-engined Cotton produced between 1923 and 1926, similar to the model which won the Junior TT in 1923 in the hands of Stan Woods

Left: Derek Minter this time on the Starmaker-powered Cotton Conquest at the 1965 Castle Coombe 500-mile race for production machines. Derek, co riding with Peter Inchley, won at 75.29mph

Below: an artist's impression of a racing Cotton, 1932 vintage

R. Haby

premises had been built for the wartime production of aero engine parts; now renamed Vulcan Works, they remained the home of Cottons right through to the late 1960s.

Probably the make's greatest moment of glory should have come with the 1926 250cc Isle of Man TT. In the record books, Cottons finished a solid first, second, and third; but in fact, Pietro Ghersi had been second man across the line on the Italian Moto-Guzzi, and it was Gherzi's exclusion by the Auto Cycle Union, for the ghastly crime of declaring one make of sparking plug, Lodge, on his entry form but using another, Fert, for the actual race, that brought Fred Morgan up to official second place, with William Colgan inheriting third place.

From the start, the race had been a duel between Johnston and Ghersi, and both men had had their share of problems. After taking the lead, Ghersi had to stop to tighten his carburettor mounting bolts, so letting Paddy get ahead. The gap between the pair closed, only to open again, and now it was Johnston's turn to worry when the gear linkage came adrift, leaving him to struggle up the mountain climb in top gear. Eventually he did gain the chequered flag, with the Moto-Guzzi man only 20 seconds behind. After that, for the Italian to be disqualified for a technical offence seemed rough justice; but, of course, the decision was not of Cotton's making, and they had every justification for cashing in on the resulting publicity.

In 1927 came the only major change in the design of the Cotton frame, when a new headstem casting splayed the lower pair of frame main tubes more widely. This was to permit taller engines to be installed, such as a newly designed overhead-camshaft Blackburne unit, or a 500cc vee-twin JAP, the valve gear of which could now protrude upwards between the frame rails.

The racing heyday of the small factories employing proprietary power units drew to a close at the end of the 1920s. Now, victory went to the bigger firms with the cash to finance development of frames and power units. Cottons were not quite done, however, and there were occasional successes such as the setting up of a dozen world records in 1935, to keep the name before the public.

For the road rider, the very accommodating frame layout permitted Cottons to offer a wide variety of models, from a 150cc side-valve in the cost-conscious depression years of 1931–2 to an imposing 600cc high-camshaft JAP sportster with enclosed pushrods and valve gear in 1939.

The Vulcan Works were commandeered to a large degree by the Ministry of Supply, and Bill had to condense his operations into a small corner of the premises. Nevertheless, Cotton production never quite came to a halt, and wartime contracts for 600cc sidecar outfits, for use in the oilfields of the Middle East, kept the company alive.

After World War II, Cottons seemed set to make a comeback with a 500cc vertical-twin side valve model, again JAP powered, and in an entirely new, rear-sprung frame. Only a prototype was built, and it seemed that Cottons had at last come to the end of the road. However, in 1953, two Gloucester enthusiasts stepped in to reconstitute the firm in the name of Mrs. Elizabeth (Kate) Cotton. They were Monty Denley and Pat Onions and, under the style of E. Cotton Motor Cycles, Vulcan Works swung back into action with a range of Villiers-engined roadsters. However, the famous triangulated frame was no more.

With the introduction of the 250cc Villiers Starmaker engine, Cottons came back to road-racing and, in the hands of riders such as Bill Ivy, Peter Inchley, and Derek Minter, the Cotton Telstar began to hit the headlines. It won the 250cc British Road Race Championship. in 1965. Disguised as a sports-roadster Cotton Conquest, it won the 250cc class of the Thruxton 500-mile marathon twice.

Soon the pendulum was swinging away from road models, and towards an all-competitions programme. But the factory suffered a severe blow when the last of the British proprietary engine makers, Villiers, closed down. Cottons had to seek engines abroad, and decided on the Italian-built Minarelli, initially in 175cc form, later enlarged to 220cc. This unit powered the Cotton Cavalier trials and enduro models, of which over 1,000 were built. Riders included Ian Haydon, Mark Kemp, Colin Dommett, and Rob Edwards, who won the 200cc cup in the 1969 Scottish Six Days Trial on a Cavalier.

With the redevelopment of Gloucester city centre, the ancestral home in Quay Street had to be vacated, and new premises were found in a former bakery at Stratton Road, Gloucester. It was from there, late in 1976, that Cottons announced their return to the road-racing scene, with an interesting water-cooled two-stroke model, this time engined by Rotax, of Austria. Initial customer reaction was very favourable, and, especially at club-race level, the new Cotton 250cc Model LCRS is being seen around more and more. The late Bill Cotton would have been proud.   FG

Below: Brian Hutchinson has no time to take in the scenery as he concentrates on the job in hand. He is riding a 175cc Minarelli-engined machine on the 1971 Scott Trial

Right: A rare outing for a Coventry Eagle 250cc ohc JAP-engined bike

Full Cycle

The Coventry Eagle company began and ended its days producing bicycles, but its reputation was founded on highly refined motor cycles

Although the Coventry-Eagle company achieved its greatest fame in the 1920s and 1930s, the firm, in fact, had been established in Victorian times as a cycle manufacturer, with works in Lincoln Street, Coventry, building machines under the 'Royal Eagle' trademark. At the 1897 National Cycle Show, they exhibited a 'Royal Eagle' gentleman's cycle, 'strongly built to carry heavy mails . . . as used by the Government in foreign postal service . . . fitted with tropical cushion tyres'. Another novelty of that year was the Gent's Mountezi cycle – 'built low to enable machine being mounted and started from a standing position'.

Early in the new century, Coventry-

337

Eagle built their first motor cycle. Little more than a strengthened pedal cycle with added power, it did have the unusual feature of a long wheelbase for stability, achieved by bringing the top tube and down tube almost together at the top of the steering head, which was braced by tubular trusses; the forks, however, were not strengthened in any way. Power was provided by an MMC engine, a carbon copy of the popular De Dion unit, with an automatic inlet valve and surface carburettor. This was clipped ahead of the down tube in what was known as the 'Minerva position', and drove direct to the back wheel by belt; the tank, which carried the controls for the carburettor, was clipped inside the diamond of the frame.

This machine could be fitted with a trailer attachment so that the young bloods of the day could take their lady friends with them, who were seated uncomfortably in a sort of cane-bodied rickshaw which received all the dust from the rear wheel. To make matters worse, the trailer connection was a flimsy device, liable to snap in half under stress, tipping trailer and occupant backwards onto the road. The love that could survive an outing in a trailer must indeed have been enduring.

By 1903, the Coventry-Eagle had become a proper motor cycle, with braced (although unsprung) front forks and a loop frame. Longuemare spray carburettors and trembler coil ignition were standard items of the specification, and engines from $1\frac{3}{4}$hp to $3\frac{1}{2}$hp could be fitted. Various makes of power unit were available, including a $2\frac{3}{4}$hp 'genuine De Dion' and a $2\frac{1}{4}$hp Buchet.

Claimed the company: 'No guesswork about their construction. Everything is the result of years of experience. Skilful engineers and workmen build them of the finest materials'.

Although Coventry-Eagle still made trailers, with bodies either in cane or wicker, they now also offered a 'Trimo', in which the front forks were replaced by a 'fore carriage' consisting of two steerable wheels linked to the handlebars with a passenger seat between them. It was marginally more comfortable than the trailer, but the occupant of the front seat was liable to act as an impromptu buffer in a collision . . . Power for this Trimo was provided by a $2\frac{1}{4}$hp De Dion engine.

After exhibiting this range at the Agricultural Hall Show in 1903, Coventry-Eagle faded from the scene to a large extent – so much so, indeed, that in later years the company had no record of its origins, guessing motor cycle production to have started in 1905.

During World War I, a lightweight was built, using a Triumph engine in a Coventry-Eagle frame, but it was not until after the war that Coventry-Eagle really got uner way. In the spring of 1921, they were offering two new sidecar models, both with coachbuilt 'chairs' and three-speed transmission, the 500cc single $3\frac{1}{2}$hp ('All you can actually *need*') and the 5–6hp 680cc JAP V-twin ('All you can reasonably desire'), then, in the late summer came two new sporting lightweights designed by Percy Mayo, a single-geared sports model and a touring model of similar design but equipped with a Sturmey-Archer gearbox of either two or three speeds and a kickstarter.

Reviewing the new models, *Motor Cycling* commented: 'All motor cyclists do not think alike. Some want machines which can be neglected for weeks at a time without suffering much in efficiency and appearance. Others take great pride in their mounts, and like to keep them always looking very spick and span. It is for the latter class that the latest Coventry-Eagle has been designed. In the first place, everything is of the best; in this, the new machine resembles many others, notably other Coventry-Eagles. Further, wherever a little extra finish could be added with advantage to the owner, it has been done. For instance, the crankcase has been smoothed and polished, so that it not only looks very well, but can be wiped over in a moment at the end of a ride, and the dust of travel removed. The machine is also full of little but important refinements, which lend themselves to the maintenance of efficiency and help to keep it up to concert pitch'.

The power unit of the new models was a specially built 249cc JAP engine with overhead valves, aluminium piston and an unusual design of detachable cylinder head which contained the ports and valve guides, but not the valve seats. 'Therefore,' claimed its makers, 'the joint need not be made compression tight'. The rockers were operated by a single cam, and the valve gear ran on roller bearings; the big end, too, ran on roller bearings, while the main bearing was of the ball type. The exhaust manifold was liberally be-finned: 'this improves the silence by cooling the gases from the earliest possible moment, which reduces the pressure, and it also has the advantage of preventing the plated exhaust pipe from being blued by the heat'.

The sporting model was intended for racing and hill-climb use, and had single-speed chain drive, using a Coventry duplex chain for reliability, although one would have thought belt drive was more suitable for a direct-drive machine devoid of clutch, however; an Enfield cush hub helped to take some of the harshness out of the final drive, however.

The keynote of this Coventry-Eagle was its luxury styling, though: polished aluminium wheel discs were fitted, and

there was much nickel-plating – cylinder barrel, final-drive sprocket, valve gear and valve springs, exhaust system, magneto casing . . .

A bulbous-nosed saddle-tank similar in appearance to that of the Brough-Superior was fitted, and caused much favourable comment in that era of almost universal flat-tanks; like the rest of the machine it was painted black, although in this case it was a matt finish, while the frame and mudguards were glossy. Cast aluminium number plates and an eagle mascot on the steering head completed the specification.

It seems as though the same machine, HP 3015, served as the prototype for both single-speed and geared models, as the rear part of the frame, which carried the gearbox, was attached by lugs, and was obviously interchangeable. Although this particular model – known as the S 25 – was not long-lived, it set the style for Coventry-Eagles for some years to come. Also included in the 1922 line-up were the TS1, a $2\frac{1}{2}$hp single-speed two-stroke, the S29, a $2\frac{3}{4}$hp model with a 293cc JAP engine, the S35, with a 3hp, 350cc JAP engine, the sporting S50, with a $3\frac{1}{2}$hp, 500cc JAP and a three-speed V-

BRIAN WATSON

twin, the 5/6hp C68, with a 680cc JAP, intended for sidecar haulage.

By the following year, the range had changed extensively: there was now a new ultra-lightweight, the 1¾hp S15; the S29, with its chain-cum-belt final drive was retained, as was the S35; there was a new 348cc model, the S34, with a Blackburne engine and all-chain drive, plus the C55 Big Single, powered by a 4¼hp, 550cc JAP, with three speeds, clutch and kick starter. Heading the range was a new big twin, the 8hp Super Sports Solo, with a 960cc JAP engine, obviously intended to appeal to the sporting rider who wanted, but could not afford, a Brough-Superior. A year later, Coventry-Eagle were offering an even more sporty V-twin, the ohv Flying-8, alongside the Super Sports. The great Bert Le Vack raced one of these at Brooklands, using specially tuned JAP engines.

The selection of 350cc models in the 1924 line-up seemed to be too much of a good thing, for there were two sports models, one with an ohv JAP, the other with an ohv Blackburne, and two touring models, with sidevalve versions of the same power units; all had three-speed

gearboxes and all-chain drive. The smallest model was now a 293cc JAP-engined machine.

A similar range was continued for several years, although there were some price reductions – and consequent losses in the standard of finish. Coventry-Eagle, who had once tried to cater for the luxury end of the market, were now aiming in the opposite direction. It must be admitted, however, that the 1928 350cc touring sidevalve, at 35 guineas, represented excellent value for money. Nor was this the cheapest model in the range, for 'the sensation of the Show' at Olympia in 1927 was a two-stroke Villiers-engined lightweight at 28 guineas, which featured a pressed-steel frame.

By 1928, there were four Coventry-Eagle models with the pressed-steel frame, which was to become a distinctive feature of the marque. These were the E21, with a 147cc Villiers two-stroke, the E23 and E25 Super-Sports, both with 175cc Villiers two-strokes, and the 200cc four-stroke E27. The rest of the range consisted of the E31 sidevalve, the ohv 350cc E44 and the sidevalve 350cc E45, the ohv 350cc twin-port E46 'Flying-350', the 500cc sidevalve E50, the 500cc ohv

Above: Coventry Eagle's 250cc Pullman of 1936 featured a sturdy pressed-steel frame and forks which had taken ten years to develop

twin-port 'Flying-500' E55, and two 'Flying-8' models, the 996cc four-cam E150 and the 996cc ohv E160. Prices ranged from £25 for the E21 to £110 for the E160.

The 1929 Olympia Show saw some alterations to this line-up: the 147 and 175cc touring models remained, while there were now two 196cc two-stroke models, a touring and a sports, both with electric lighting as standard – it was an extra on all the other Coventry-Eagles apart from the 998cc ohv V-twin. Then there were 300cc and 490cc touring models, a 348cc Sports with a twin-port ohv Sturmey-Archer GPRM engine, and a 496cc Sports with a twin-port ohv Sturmey-Archer DPRO power unit which, like its smaller stablemate, had sight-feed lubrication and an internal flywheel. There were two JAP-engined sports machines, of 345cc and 491cc respectively, plus, of course, the big-twin.

This basic range continued into 1931,

although the two smallest two-stroke models were dropped, and the 196cc bikes acquired the names 'Wonder' and 'Super-Sports', while the power units were now inclined in the frame instead of being vertical.

With the Depression at its height (or depth!) in 1931, Coventry-Eagle now turned their full attention to economy. The 996cc JAP model disappeared, leaving the 500cc H55 as the biggest model in the range. There were now three distinct 350s, the three-speed H40 and H45 and the four-speed H44, only one 196cc two-stroke, the H22, and two 147cc models, the two-speed H18, which retailed for only 19 guineas, and the

three-speed H19, which cost £23 10s. Finally, there was the smallest-ever Coventry-Eagle, the 98cc H16 two-stroke autocycle, which cost only 16 guineas.

Low-priced uniformity was the order of the day by 1933, with a choice of only two engine capacities, 148cc two-stroke and 250cc two or four-stroke models, and it was three years before 350cc and 500cc four-stroke sporting models were once again listed. That same year, Coventry-Eagle brought out the final incarnation of the pressed-steel frame, pressed-steel forks design that they had been developing for a decade. This was the 250cc Pullman two-stroke, with generous mud-guarding and legshields in unit with the

frame.

However, Coventry-Eagle's bicycling side was now enjoying a resurgence, thanks to the mid 1930s passion for hiking and cycling and, although the company resumed cycle manufacture after the war, motor cycle production ceased in 1939.   DBW

Below: the Coventry Eagle B33 of 1926, a 300cc JAP-engined machine with an Albion gearbox, which evolved into the C33 in 1927, the D31 in 1928 and E35 in 1929

TAKING IT IN TURNS

STEAM LOCOMOTIVE PRACTICE INSPIRED some of the first petrol-driven vehicles, notably Edward Butler's 1884 Tricycle, in which the crankshaft also constituted the driving wheel spindle. Since then, there have been very few exceptions in motor cycling to the general rule that the crankshaft is the engine's power output shaft, for it is the final component in the link mechanism whereby the linear motion of the engine's pistons is converted to rotary motion for more convenient transmission to the driving wheels. The essential feature of the crankshaft is a number of eccentrics (otherwise cranks or throws) which are linked to the pistons by connecting rods furnished with suitable bearings at each end to permit the necessary articulation. As the crankshaft rotates in its own main bearings, the eccentrics (the varying portions of which are called crankpins) rotate in a circle whose mean diameter is equal to the piston stroke.

The number of throws is not necessarily equal to the number of cylinders: in some kinds of engine configuration, two connecting rods may bear on one crankpin. The V-twin provides an example, and in essentials the 360° parallel twin is the same, although the single crankpin is divided into two by a central balance-weight that also functions as a flywheel. Balancing is an important consideration, and is achieved by fixing counter-weights opposite the crank throws, or at some other angle as in some six-cylinder designs. Their object is not only to eliminate or minimise vibration, but also to relieve the shaft of bending loads. Resistance to bending is also improved by making the shaft of large diameter, so that the main and crankpin bearing portions overlap. This tends to make the shaft very heavy, increasing main bearing loads and the rotational inertia of the shaft; hollow crankpins are an antidote, but the complications of sealing them to contain the necessary internal flow of lubricating oil are generally too costly to be popular in motor cycle production. Lubricating oil is fed to big-end bearings through the interior of the shaft, and the internal cavities must be carefully shaped to avoid oil sludge clogging the oilways under the influence of centrifugal force.

Stiffness of construction is also important in resisting torsional vibration. All crankshafts are subject to this, each shaft having its own natural frequency of torsional vibration which must not be allowed to coincide with the frequency of impulses from the pistons, lest the shaft go into resonance and break. The longer and thinner the crankshaft and the greater the number of pistons impelling it, the greater is the shaft's susceptibility to torsional oscillation, which may demand the addition of a torsional damper (usually a small flywheel with a torsionally resilient or partially free hub) to the nose of the crankshaft to prevent torsional flutter from developing. A short crankshaft is stiffer in torsion than a long one, hence its natural frequency is higher and may more readily be set beyond the normal working range of the engine. A single-cylinder engine is virtually immune from problems of this nature; at the other extreme, a six-cylinder in-line engine is particularly sensitive to it. This is why a six-cylinder design with four main bearings is to be preferred for high-speed work to one with seven main bearings, although the latter (despite its greater length) will be less affected by bending loads that can produce a rumble at low speeds in a four-bearing engine. The simplest and most desirable measure is to avoid the practice common in car engineering of taking the power from one end of the crankshaft: in motor cycles, this is seldom

Below: a single-cylinder type crankshaft from a Honda C50. The full circle webs act as a flywheel. Full circle webs on a two stroke machine are useful for filling crankcase volume to aid mixture transfer

convenient from a transmission point of view if the transversely set crankshaft has to serve more than three cylinders, and it is usual for the power to be abstracted from the middle of a four- or six-cylinder crankshaft. By doing so, the effective length of free shaft is halved and the natural frequency of torsional oscillations is doubled, which is usually sufficient to eliminate the problem. Nothing so elegant can be achieved with in-line engines having an odd number of cylinders, for the shaft will have to be unevenly divided; nevertheless, there are several three-cylinder engines featuring a power take-off between the middle cylinder and one of those flanking it, and similarly asymmetric measures were adopted by Honda for their five-cylinder 125cc racer in 1965.

One-piece crankshafts with three, five, or six throws are costly to produce, and therefore anathema to the motor cycle manufacturer. It is particularly so if the shafts are machined from forgings, leading to some interesting production tricks. The three-throw shaft of the Triumph Trident, to quote one instance, was forged with all its throws lying in the same plane, and subsequently subjected to powerful mechanical tweaks which twisted it to leave the crankpins disposed as they should be at 120° intervals. In the three-cylinder Laverda, the crankpins remain in one plane, and the engine runs with uneven firing intervals. In three-cylinder two-stroke engines, the need for roller bearings and a built-up crankshaft eliminate the problem.

Crankshaft design is governed above all by the type of bearings chosen. Plain journal bearings, relying on an hydro-dynamic oil film to keep the bearing surfaces apart, were once despised by motor cyclists but made substantial inroads when vertical twins became popular and are now extensively used in multi-cylinder four-strokes. Such bearings demand meticulous surface finishing and, according to the nature of the actual bearing material, may require special hardening treatment (such as nitriding) of the shaft, which must then be of a material amenable to this treatment. Where ball or roller bearings are preferred, it is possible to split these so as to retain a one-piece crankshaft, but it is far more common for the shaft to be built up from a number of smaller pieces, the bearings being fitted to the appropriate parts before assembly. A built-up crankshaft is often less robust than a one-piece shaft, because it is difficult to arrange for the crankpins and main bearing journals to overlap (although substantially shouldered crankpins are a palliative), but it has a natural ability to damp out torsional flutter at some risk of fretting corrosion, and is often chosen because it allows a much stronger connecting rod to be used: the split big-end eye of the rod appropriate to a one-piece shaft is always a source of weakness.

The means of assembling a built-up shaft vary from simple interference fits (in which a crankpin may be pressed into a hole in a crank web, or chilled and then allowed to expand into it) to complex bolted assemblies relying on radial serrations (as in the Hirth crankshaft of the V8 Moto Guzzi racer of the 1950s) to keep the parts in their proper relationships. In any case, the process relies on skilled fitting, and usually makes the dismantling of the engine more problematic.

There are objections to the practice of interposing a main bearing between each pair of adjacent crank throws. Torsional flutter has already been mentioned, but there are also such matters as greater frictional losses and sheer expense. In the case of an in-line four-cylinder engine, there is a good case for setting the shaft in four main bearings, the central one being omitted to make way for a bob-weight; but as we have seen, it is now common motor cycle practice to provide a power offtake between the innermost cylinders, in which case the number of main bearings may well be increased to six. In any case, the modern fashion for engines of relatively large bore and short stroke encourages a multiplicity of main bearings: the length of the shaft is governed by the irreducible length of the cylinder block (the distance between cylinder centres being

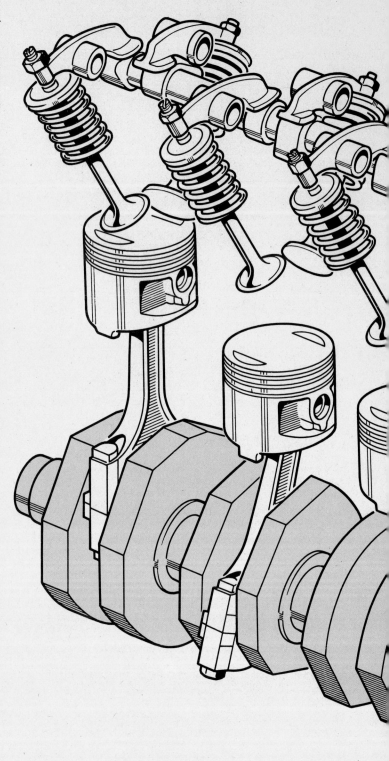

Above: this diagram shows the relative positions of the major internal components of a Benelli six-cylinder engine. The crankshaft itself is the coloured assembly and it incorporates the sprocket which drives the valve gear

necessarily great in an air-cooled engine) and only by having a full complement of main bearings can the shaft be protected from bending loads. It then becomes convenient to feed oil to each crankpin from an adjacent main bearing. There have been a few engines in which separate oil pumps fed the main bearings and, via an end-to-end oilway drilled through the length of the shaft, the big-end bearings: this would make it feasible, although it has seldom if ever been done in a motor cycle, to cater for the different requirements of roller main bearings and plain big-ends, which would be the ideal arrangement.

In more conventional multi-cylinder practice, where oil is introduced to the crankshaft (and thus to the big-end bearings) from the main bearings, the plain bearings of the latter are drilled and have a groove to carry the oil around the whole circumference of the journal so that the lubricant will be able to enter the crankshaft drillings regardless of rotational position. The provision of oilways in a built-up crankshaft is not so easy to arrange without introducing a number of stress-raisers that might corrupt the design; but such shafts are almost

invariably associated with rolling element bearings which need much less oil, and which can usually be supplied in adequate quantities by spray, mist, or oil slingers which are specially shaped sheet metal saucers which centrifuge the oil away from the shaft and fling it at the big-end bearings. LJKS

*Left: the crankshaft and connecting rods from a
SS125A Honda*

*Below: an exploded diagram of a typical built up crankshaft
assembly. The individual parts are as listed below:*
A *Gudgeon pin circlip*
B *Gudgeon pin*
C *Piston with bushes*
D *Expander ring*
E *Piston rings*
F *Connecting rod bush*
G *Connecting rod*
H, J *Crankpin plugs*
I *Crankpin*
K *Rollers for crankpin*
L *Engine sprocket*
M *Engine sprocket washer*
N *Engine sprocket nut*
O, Z *Woodruff keys*
P, R, W, Y *Ball bearings for crankshaft*
Q, X *Driveshaft ball bearing distance piece*
S *Driving shaft left hand*
T, V *Cover plate for driveshaft balance weight*
U *Drive shaft right hand*

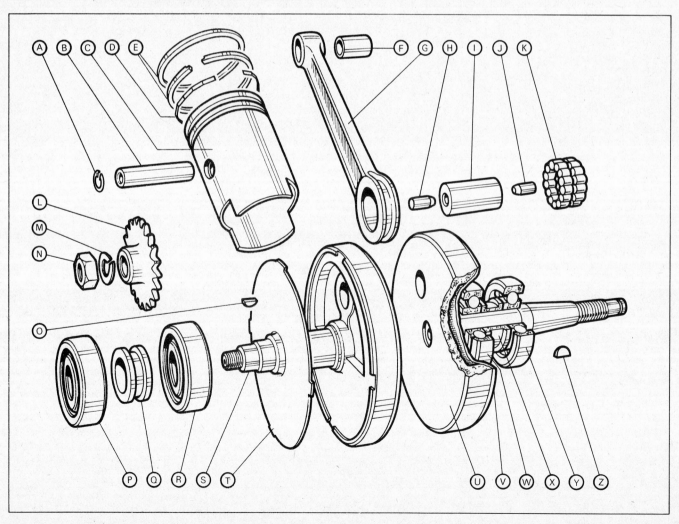

Dave 'TV' Croxford began his bike racing career on London's North Circular Road in the days of the Ace cafe but, after losing his licence, he decided to try his luck on the circuits. His first rides were as a sidecar passenger which brought some success and much discomfort, but he soon went solo. With clubman's meetings hard to find in the early 1960s, he drove 450 miles from his Ruislip home to Charter Hall in Scotland for his first unsuccessful attempt with his £350 Manx Norton. In 1963, he won his first clubman's event at Oulton Park and, the following year, 'got serious' with a G50 Matchless. On one occasion,

a crankcase split beneath him and, out of the blue, tuner Charlie Oakley arrived and offered Dave his own competitive machinery. This partnership lasted several years and, after winning a nationally televised race in 1966, Dave collected his first British Championship title the following year; at the time, he was one of the first riders using a front disc brake.

1968 was to be his most successful year, winning the 500cc Championship and, for the first time ever, three circuit titles – King of Brands, Master of Mallory and Lord of Lydden. In 1969, he was again 500cc British champion.

Dave's move from Matchless to the Seeley machines, with revamped G50 engines, was followed by a period on Norton twins, most notably for sponsor Gus Kuhn. In 1971, he shared the winning bike in the Thruxton 500 mile race, a victory which he repeated the following year, even though he had to finish on foot, pushing his 'dead' Norton across the line.

When John Player Team Norton needed another rider to replace the injured John Cooper, Croxford was chosen for his first works ride; the name on his machine's white fairing was later changed to 'Crashford' by his mechanics! He stayed with them until

The Single-minded Racer

1976, but that first season's success was never to be repeated. Since winning the '73 British 750cc Championship and a few races in '74, the Nortons were outclassed. When John Player left Norton and the Cosworth Challenge engine appeared, Dave was the last of the works riders, but two years with the new machine, 1975 and '76, saw him start only eight races, most of which he failed to finish. While every attempt was made to sort out the machines, Dave maintains that the Challenge's 100bhp engine was not suitable for road racing.

'Crockers' or 'Crockett' as he is sometimes called, has always been a 'four-stroke man': during his best years, everyone rode identical British machinery, and Dave points out that financially things were a lot easier in those days. The Norton, AJS and Matchless singles that were around made it possible for a good up-and-coming rider to mix it with the champions, but he was one of the first to speak out about the 'Big Engine Bandits': riders using oversize motors to keep ahead of the field.

Croxford has, on occasion, raced two-stroke machinery, as in 1976 when he borrowed Percy Tait's 500cc Suzuki at Snetterton, but that ride ended when water got into the works. 'Two strokes

are too expensive', he quipped. 'It cost me £200 just to borrow it.' Indeed, the expense of racing in the mid 1970s is one thing that Dave found hard to live with. In the days of the singles, very few spares were needed during a season, just plugs, sprockets and a couple of tyres.

Never a regular on the Isle of Man, although he finished eleventh in his first TT in 1965, Dave returned ten years later to win the Production TT with Alex George on the legendary Triumph, *Slippery Sam*, a machine which had won the race four times previously.

Dave had won the 1974 Yuletide race at Brands Hatch but, after being picked for the '75 TranAtlantic Trophy team, he did not have much luck with the Norton, falling off at Mallory Park and Brands.

The following season saw his mount last only the first few laps of the '76 match race series and Dave dropped out of the British team and announced he was quitting Nortons, although he did in fact, return later in the season. Meanwhile, he had been keeping his hand in with rides in Coup d'Endurance races on the French Japauto machines. The bikes with their works Honda sixteen-valve engines took Dave and his partners to a ninth place in the Bol d'Or 24 hour race and a third at the

Thruxton 500.

At different times in his life Dave has been employed as a glazier, engineer, painter and decorator, poodle parlour attendant, used-car salesman, sometime TV personality, comedian and general entertainer. Always light hearted, some of his stories can stand retelling: like the time ambulance men removed his boots after a crash to find nail varnish on his toes, or when he waved at Barry Sheene while sliding backwards along the track, or even the classic Isle of Man remark about being passed by a pig – a sad comment on the performance of his Norton.

While Dave has had his unlucky spells and even periods of retirement, he has also been fortunate in keeping his injury score down with only a few stitches needed after a grand total of 189 crashes.

In 1977, the 'Crock's' career as a professional racer is coming to an end. The year may see him in some long-distance races, but his used-car business is taking up most of his time, although he does manage to put in some work on his son Steve's schoolboy scrambler. GE

Previous page: Dave Croxford on John Player Norton, Silverstone 1974, and below, at Mallory in 1971

All or Nothing

England's speedway hero of late 1976 was World Champion Peter Collins, the brilliant Belle Vue rider, but 1977 would see him coming under intense pressure from Australia's number one, the equally brilliant Phil Crump. Darling of the 'Down Under' shale fans, Phil has the same sort of adulation in his own country as Collins does here. And he is dedicating himself to wrestling from Collins the one title that matters so much in speedway – the World Championship itself.

Crump, one of the toughest riders in the sport, intended to redress the balance in the world championship and do the same for Australia, as Collins did for England. England had been in the world championship doldrums since 1962, when the late Peter Craven became the last Englishman to win the coverted crown. But an Australian had not won the title since 1952 when Jack Young won at Wembley.

The 'Mildura Marvel', nicknamed af-ter his home town in Victoria, made his first world final appearance in 1975 at Wembley when he tied on 10 points with Collins behind that year's champion the Dane Ole Olsen, Anders Michanek, John Louis and Ivan Mauger.

His greatest moment of triumph came in 1976, however, when, in front of 100,000 people in the Slaski stadium, Chorzow, Poland, he became the first 'Aussie' to step up onto the top-three rostrum since 1958, when Aub Lawson came third. His brilliant display saw him take that third spot, behind Englishmen Peter Collins and Malcolm Simmons.

For 1977, Crump hoped to be even better, and started to find what had been missing in his approach to the sport – professionalism. He has always shown he has the great skill to make a top liner but something in his basic make up has let him down. He let himself down in organisation – so important when one night he might be turning out in Wales for his British league team Newport, then having to fit in a continental trip or two before returning to more league action. So, he approached the man who aided four times World Champion Ivan Mauger for so many years, Peter Oakes, a freelance journalist and sometime team manager of Exeter.

In the toughest speedway league in the world, Crump finished fifth overall, headed only by John Louis, Ivan Mauger, Ole Olsen and Peter Collins. But, who scored the most points? It was that man Crump: top man Louis scored only 315 actual race points in league matches, while Crump had the astounding total of 434 points! In fact, he was the only rider in the country to grab over 400 points in the season, and Crump even admitted that he got bogged down in dealing with bookings and all the intricate deal-ings that have to be done in the back-ground to make a living. With Oakes looking after the paperwork, 1977 pro-mised to be better.

The son of an Australian grape farmer,

Above: the ambitious Phil Crump, seen leading Malcolm Simmons during the 1977 World Final at Slaski Stadium, Poland, when he finished third behind Simmons and Peter Collins

Crump has formed a unique partnership in speedway and maybe in sport altogether, in that he rides with his father-in-law, Neil Street! At 45, Street in 1977 is one of the oldest riders still active but, more importantly for Crump, he is an engineering maestro.

For, it was Street, and not the British Weslake company, that started the four-valve engine revolution in speedway. For many years, the Czech Jawa engine had been the best engine available and had been unchallenged. Then, Street and an old school chum, Ivan Tighe, got together in Australia and worked out a four-valve Jawa conversion. It worked like a dream and, for the whole of 1975, Crump and Street had the only two four-valve motors. The new powerful engine astounded the speedway world with its terrific pulling power off the start, which is so important. Both Street and Crump reeled off maximum after maximum at the start of the 1975 season using the maestro's engines and, in

Crump's hands, it had its first major track success at the *Daily Express* Spring Classic meeting at Wimbledon. Now, literally dozens of the top riders in the world are using Street motors, while the man behind the project continues to develop them further.

Like so many Australasians before him, Crump came to England to seek his fortune, and he did not have to wait long. After having the meeting rides at his local track, Mildura, in 1970, the teen-ager came to England in 1971 to ride for Second Division team Crewe, and finished with a distinguished near-nine-point average.

In 1972, he came top of the Second Division averages with 11.09 points and won his first major honour, the prestige Division Two British Riders championship. That same year, he had 19 outings with First Division King's Lynn – and scored his first major league maximum. However, his career was destined to continue at Newport where he has been

Above: Ivan Mauger of New Zealand and Exeter leads Phil Crump and Egon Muller of West Germany during the 1976 World Final in Poland

virtually unbeatable.

Australian championship, Victorian championship, Australian long track championship, Victorian short track championship, Golden Helmet match race championship, Crump has won them all. And in 1976, he earned himself a piece of a world title, for he was one of the mainstays of Australia, winning the world team cup for the first time ever. Crump was one of a mighty Australian quartet who put out reigning World Champion's England in a qualifier at Ipswich and then went on to take the final at White City, from Sweden, Russia and Poland.

For 1977, Crump does not want just a piece of a world title – he wants the solo world title, and he will take some stopping. AE

Chopping & Changing

1968 was quite a busy year for motor cycling – Triumph unveiled their new generation three-cylinder super-bike, the 750cc Trident; Honda announced the coming of their own big roadster, the 70hp, four-cylinder CB750; Alf Hagon pushed the record for the British Standing Quarter Mile to 9.208 secs with a terminal speed of 155.7mph, Sammy Miller became the first official European Trials Champion and Mike Hailwood, twelve times Isle of Man TT victor, received the MBE. The TT racing programme itself was extended to include a 750cc Sidecar Class, John Player brought big-time sponsorship to road racing and Suzuki launched their attack on the world of motocross. And, in the hinterland of the United States, aspiring movie moguls Dennis Hopper and Peter Fonda were stretching a shoe-string budget from Los Angeles to New Orleans to record the exploits of two bike riding hippies who went in search of the American dream, freedom.

In contrast to the previous year, 1969 shaped-up to be something of an anti-climax. Then 'Easy Rider' hit the British cinema screen; overnight the film transformed an obscure form of American motor cycle art into a household name – the chopper had arrived, together with a whole new subculture and attendant jargon.

Ironically, 'Easy Rider' was never intended to be a bike movie. It owes this misnomer to the rash of second rate American made motor cycle films that broke onto the cinema circuits following its general release.

Motor cycles, tough guys and highway banditry were popular themes of the late sixties American media and the film industry saw 'Easy Rider's' gleaming chopped Harley-

Below: a showbike, impractical for road use because of its design, fitted with a 500cc Honda motor

Davidsons as their green light for 'Go'. But no end of jaw-busting violence and immaculately burnished custom machinery – not even guest appearances by the biggest baddies of them all, the then notorious Hell's Angels – could redress the shallow plots and monosyllabic scripts. The motor cycle movies came and went, but 'Easy Rider', with its breathtaking American landscapes, contemporary soundtrack and two of the most beautiful machines ever to be committed to celluloid, lived on.

The cinema had given the British motor cyclist a taste of life on the other side of the Atlantic, a place where the sun always shone, the air was clean and the roads stretched on for ever. Even more, it had shown him that American motor cycles were not all like the heavily laden monsters the Highway Patrolmen rode in imported TV police dramas, or the bizarre spotlight and wrought-iron bedecked show bikes that occasionally crept into the pages of the British motor cycle press.

On the west coast of America a style had evolved that reduced the bulging production Harley Davidson to its basic components, transforming the gargantuan into a lean, lithe missile. The machines we saw in 'Easy Rider' epitomised that style, a mixture of practicality and automotive folk-art.

The style had an obvious and immediate appeal but, presented as he was with a *fait accompli*, it was some time before the British biker could resolve what he had seen in his own terms. Consequently, the first European choppers, built by European motorcyclists with backgrounds and traditions so totally removed from their American counterparts, were barely recognisable imitations of a fascinating, yet completely misunderstood, ideal.

If we look at the American production motor cycles of the early 1950s, the apparently indisciplined force of chopping takes on a little meaning. Following the collapse of the legendary Indian Motocycle Company in 1951, and the cessation of all manufacture at the Springfield, Massachusetts, works in 1953, the US motor cycle industry was represented almost exclusively by the Harley-Davidson Motor Company of Milwaukee. With the exception of a 125cc lightweight, derived from the same pre-war DWK design as the BSA Bantam, Harley-Davidson's two major offerings were of enormous capacity and weight, out-dated in concept and expensive to buy. By comparison, British-built machines (notably Triumphs which made incredibly rapid inroads into the American market at this time), were light and manageable. They performed as well as, if not better than, Harleys of almost twice their engine capacity, and cost between $150 and $180 less.

To compete with the British threat to their market domination, Harley-Davidson tried unsuccessfully to raise the existing import duty of 10 per cent on foreign made motor cycles to 40 per cent, and asked for the imposition of a quota system whereby the number of imported machines should be a given percentage of the number that they, themselves, could manufacture and sell. Harley riders, on the other hand, opted to modify their bikes along more competitive lines and beat the 'limeys' on equal terms.

Triumph's 650cc, twin-cylinder Thunderbird, early mainstay of the American invasion, tipped the scales in standard trim at 397lb. Its efficient, compactly designed motor developed 35bhp producing a top speed in the region of 102mph, and a standing quarter mile acceleration figure of 15.4 seconds. Harley Davidson's two 'modern' overhead-valve V-twins had engine capacities of 61 cu. in. (1000cc) and 74 cu. in. (1200cc) developing 43 and 53bhp respectively. Both machines weighed slightly less than 600lb stock; the 61 had a top speed of between 95–100mph; the 74 could manage a healthy 110 although over the standing quarter it was still a good two seconds slower than the Triumph.

In the absence of specialised engine tuning parts, the most obvious route to better performance was by reducing weight.

Traditionally, American motor cycles were styled for long distance touring and comfort; mudguards were vast and deeply valanced, wide section tyres and broad, tractor-style saddles compensated for crude or, in the case of pre-1958 Harleys, only partial suspension. Handlebars were incredibly wide and sweeping, tall windshields, saddlebags and crash bars were the accepted norm, and the rider's feet rested not on pegs, as was the European practice, but on long, wide boards.

By stripping-off all the unnecessary paraphernalia and substituting lighter items for essential parts, the Harley buff could reduce his machine's overall weight by as much as 100lb. Small solo seats borrowed from the dirt racers of the period, shortened, and in the case of the front wheel, the often total absence of mudguarding, high level exhausts, narrow Flanders 'cowhorn' bars and 18 or 19 inch wheels transformed a big 'hog' into an equal match for all but the fastest British bikes. These early abbreviated V-twins were called 'bobbed-jobs'; the term for cutting back weight and unwanted equipment – 'chopping' – was borrowed from the hot rodders.

Once established, the chopped motor cycle developed along lines that veered further and further away from its original concept. Wheels had been turning back at the Harley-Davidson factory, and in October 1953 an up-dated version of the 750cc side-valve model K was announced. The K had been in production for only two years, but despite many interesting features – four-speed gearbox in unit with the motor, double loop frame with a slimmer version of H-D's Hydra-Glide telescopic forks and swinging arm rear suspension – the early examples were way down on power. The new model KH featured a capacity boost to 883cc, a power output of 38bhp at 5000rpm and a top speed of over 100mph. Harley fans no longer had to rework their mounts before they could blow the British imports into the weeds.

The 61 series was dropped that same year but there was still a place in American motor cycling for a top capacity V-twin so the 74 soldiered on. It remained the mainstay of the respectable and widespread touring motor cycle clubs and in its chopped, cut-down guise, it became the darling of a new and growing breed of twentieth century outlaw.

Just as the silver screen had brought choppers across the Atlantic in 1969, some sixteen years earlier it had proclaimed the message of wild, two-wheeled power and massive anti-social behaviour to America itself. In 1947, a small rural town in the foothills of the Diablo mountains in California celebrated Independence Day with, among other things, a motor cycle hill climb. Over 4000 bikers arrived to spectate and take part in what was an official, AMA (American Motor cycle Association) sanctioned event, but, because several of the clubs that turned up were not affiliated to the AMA, they were prevented from taking part. That night the race-goers descended on the town, Hollister, to eat, drink and recount the day's happenings. As might be expected, there was a certain amount of lawless behaviour and several people were arrested by the local police. As might equally be expected, the news media seized upon the juicier aspects of the affair and Hollister, hoodlums and motor cycles became instant matters for national concern.

The AMA sprang to the defence of the good name of motor cycling, condemning the vandalism and placing the blame firmly on the shoulders of the 'outlawed' clubs. Hollywood, on the other hand, recorded the incident for posterity in the motion picture 'The Wild One', strengthening the stand of the 'outlaw' clubs and, unwittingly, in the performances of Marlon Brando and Lee Marvin, giving America its first representation of the type of two-wheeled dropout who was to appear almost ten years after the film's release in 1953.

In the years following Hollister and 'The Wild One', outlaw motor cycle clubs spread throughout the United States. Unable to shed the stigma of those early days and facing almost total rejection from the rest of society, they established a cult

A chopped hog of the mid 1960s, similar to the subject of Dave Mann's paintings and based on a stretched Harley-Davidson frame, with 80 cubic inch side-valve engine, long springer forks and peanut petrol tank

of their own based on a total disregard for everything that Western civilisation held dear. The one valued possession of the motor cyclist was his machine and that, almost without exception, was a chopped Harley 74. It had to be – like the gunslinger's Colt 45, the 74 was the biggest and the most powerful.

High performance remained of primary importance, but gradually, and most notably where biking rubbed shoulders with the growing hip culture of the West Coast, the task of reworking a bike lost more and more of the early, indiscriminate, cavalier approach in favour of a conscious effort to create a truly unique machine. Allied to the thriving hot rod industry of the mid-sixties, outlaw motor cycle dealers began to show an alarming lack of respect for everything that had gone before by way of motor cycle engineering. The hot rodders folk hero, Ed 'Big Daddy' Roth, creator of the 'Surfermobile', 'The Moon Car' and 'The Beatnik Bandit', to name but a few, turned his attentions exclusively to building custom bikes, and the fruits of his, and others, labours appeared with increasing regularity amongst the rows of painstakingly remodelled four-wheelers at the custom shows.

By the mid-fifties teenage American life revolved almost exclusively around the automobile; they rebuilt them, burnished them, lived in them, loved in them, ate in them, watched movies from them and wrote songs about them.

Nation-wide hot rod shows, following the lead of the Oakland, California, Roadster Show which began in 1949, staged year-round displays of the latest and slickest fads on four wheels. Motor cycles generally, and choppers especially, were never really in the running although Eastern and Southern States stylists did eventually manage to get a foot in the door.

Above: the café racer aims to get his machine looking like a road racer, but bestows upon it an exotic paint job and tinted screen

Top left: a Harley dresser; no chopping here, but great care is taken over the finish, including the wrought iron decoration

Left: no kitchen sink, but all the lights work on this ultimate dresser, which is even fitted with television, radio and cassette player

But their machines were a far cry from the West Coast bikes, decked out as they were with acres of chrome plated iron-work, spotlamps and tail-lamps, fender trimmings and crash bar trimmings, wheel embellishers, fish tail exhaust extensions, deeply upholstered dual seats and wide, white walled tyres. West Coast bikes may not have been topics for polite conversation, but East Coast bikes – 'dressers', or 'garbage waggons' as the outlaws preferred to call them – were a joke. It took characters like Roth, crazy auto-artists frustrated by the pace of the rest of the hot rod world, yet recognised leaders none the less, to set the record straight.

Presented for the first time in the respectable surroundings of the car shows, choppers were no longer a taboo subject. Society's avant garde took to them instantly. Naturally, though, they had to go one step beyond and dress them up; at first a little, and then a lot. So much so, in fact, that even the builders acknowledged them as unrideable and consequently left out the internal mechanics of their engines, retaining only a chrome and alloy shell. Anything went – fantasy was, and still is, infinite. Roth, one-time upholder

and uncrowned king of the motor cycle underground, moved on to the outworld of moneyed citizens. 'Chopping is the latest addition to folk art in America', he stated; but his credibility was shattered permanently and he faded from the scene. He left his mark though, not the least in that one aspect that sets the chopper apart from the crowd – the long, extended front fork. During his happier days with the outlaws, Roth had operated a large scale mail order business selling do-it-yourself chopper booklets, T-shirts and biker posters. The man he employed to paint the posters was a Kansas City artist called David Manning, himself a dedicated member of the chopper fraternity. Manning began working for Roth in 1966 and his wild, fantasised renderings of outlaw life became so popular that he eventually produced no less than 28 different designs.

The bikes in the 'Dave Mann' paintings were outrageous by the standards of the time, but they fired the imaginations of folk already aware of the new, more individual approach of true custom building. The chopper was still, basically, a bobbed-job; extensive use of chrome plate and vivid paint designs were an adopted legacy from Ed Roth's hot rod days; high-rising 'apehanger' handlebars, tall passenger grab rails called 'sissy bars', and upswept exhaust systems were really nothing more than extensions, literally, of the original 'look'. Small capacity petrol tanks liberated from a variety of mini-engined two-wheelers had replaced the 74's four gallon factory item, a Highway Patrol spotlamp lit the way, the front brake was completely discarded and the stock five inch front tyre replaced with an ultra-narrow three. Alterations to either frame or steering geometry were unheard of other than for minor increases in ground clearance.

353

Above: a Harley Davidson 1200cc shovel-head, customised in classic fat-bob style

Above right: a typical British chopper, with a 650 Triumph engine fitted to a moulded frame with a small tank

Dave Mann depicted the chopper as a long, lean warhorse, a bike that looked as though it was going fifty miles-an-hour just parked by the kerb. He achieved the effect by exaggerating the perspective in his paintings, stretching the bikes out with enormously long front forks and spindly frames wrapped around a massive V-twin motor. He had given the chopper its breakthrough.

Wanting the 'Dave Mann look' was one thing; achieving it was another. Few owner-builders had the facilities or the expertise to extend a front end or give a frame additional degrees of rake on their own. In any case, simply modifying existing parts was no longer sufficient to meet the demand for individuality. A new custom industry was created, this time for motor cycles, producing everything from chromed spike nuts to complete bike frames – even, in some cases, complete bikes.

Now to be the basis of a multi-million dollar operation, the chopper was very much 'above ground'. Nevertheless, the outlaw clubs, having survived a second and more concentrated wave of adverse publicity followed by the predictable spate of baddie biker movies already mentioned, maintained the machine's heritage while the establishment contrived to exploit every possible, and even impossible, variation on the theme. More radically modified than ever before, the outlaws still used their bikes for long, hard riding. Concessions to styling such as a long front fork were compensated for by altering the angle of the frame headstock – raking – to retain the bike's original, low, centre of gravity. Fuel tanks could not be so small that the rider had to call at every petrol station he passed. Some States, alarmed at the increasing number of strange-looking motor cycles riding their highways, enacted restrictive vehicle construction laws to kerb the madness as they had done when hot-rodding was all the rage. Handlebar heights, seat heights, fork extensions and mudguarding all came under close scrutiny. No outlaw relished spending any more time than he had to arguing with the 'law', so even his most out-landish touches were kept on the legal side of illegal.

Not so the 'straight' custom biker. By 1970 a motor cycle was as much a constituent of the stylish American household as a micro-wave oven and a video recorder for the TV in the den. A chopper, a customised motor cycle, was unquestionably one step ahead of the neighbours even though the owner probably never trusted himself on it. Show bike innovations, as impracticable in their own way as the over-laden dressers had been, found their way onto the street. Exhaust pipes towered higher than ever before, frames were stretched out front and back and forks got longer and longer. Fortunately, though, somewhere along the line the chopper industry paused and took stock of the situation before it got out of hand. Wary of further vehicle construction legislation, the custom bike magazines launched on the wave of the chopper boom put great stress on the safety aspects of machine construction.

The domination of the big Harley-Davidsons was at an end. It had remained the backbone of the movement for over thirty years but gradually foreign machines had eased it out of the limelight. For a short while it looked as though Triumphs and BSAs might be the next in line for the crown but their earlier, sound reputations were shaken by the coming of the Japanese superbikes. First Honda's four-cylinder 750 and then Kawa-saki's 900 put a new face on the world of big biking, including custom building, introducing a new era.

The Harley years left their mark; the classic lines of the old 74's rigid frame were carried through into the custom chassis for the new, swinging arm bikes; the old Harley springer front fork gave rise to a dozen or more variations on a basic theme that is still the most favoured even today. 'Chopping'

Above left: a four cylinder Honda engine in a custom frame. The swinging arm is retained, and extended front forks are substituted for the conventional variety

is no longer a faithful description of the art as a whole though. It has been absorbed into the much wider field of motor cycle customising, a field subdivided by the exponents of several varying styles.

Early bobbed-jobs, when they can be found or pieced together with authentic custom parts and innovations, are regarded with the same reverence as precious classics.

Bikes built on the outlaw principle of lean looks and high performance fall into the rather ill-defined category of the street racer, a half-way mark between the chopper proper, and a newcomer to the American scene, the cafe racer. The roughest of guide-lines for the uninitiated custom bike spotter would be that a chopper has an extended front fork of some description, a small petrol tank, a certain amount of moulding to clean up the frame lines, an intricate paint design, a high backed seat and a skinny wheel at the front and a fat one at the back.

The cafe racer, on the other hand, is a direct crib of the bikes to be seen on the road racing circuits. In the early sixties, in the days before the British motor cyclist knew anything very much about the American scene, his most coveted machine was one styled after the racers of the period. At that time several manufacturers, notably Velocette and BSA, built limited numbers of 'clubman's racers', highly tuned versions of their standard roadsters. These, together with owner-converted production machines, formed the basis of the British 'ton-up' era. Road racing equipment, lightweight aluminium petrol tanks, low fitting clip-on handlebars, rear-set footrests and the like, became a lucrative business with at first the spin-off, and soon the major demand coming from the young, would-be racers.

These youngsters spent their evenings in all-night transport cafes and coffee bars, sipping frothy cups of Espresso coffee to the blare of a rock 'n' roll jukebox. To punctuate the boredom they made an elaborate ritual of hair-raising, dare-devil rides from one cafe to the next – hence the term 'cafe racer'. However, although the cafe racer was the British equivalent of the American chopper, it never developed beyond its initial concept. Essentially it was a plaything of young men in their late teens and early twenties, snatching a few high speed thrills and spills before they settled down. Any elaboration once the style had been achieved was concentrated on the motor, there were no spray gun wizards ready to lay down a dozen coats of glittering Metalflake or Candy paint, no custom shows, no protagonists of the cafe racer art.

During the early 1960s, a parallel but counter movement emerged briefly, involving the so-called Mods, who, to the disdain of motor cyclists, rode Vespa and Lambretta motor scooters. In four years, their motorised fashions progressed from highly ornamented machines with chromed panels, luggage racks and crash-bars to riding the bare frames, bereft of all bodywork. Noisy sports silencers were mandatory, and, instead of the experience of high speed, the scooterist's aspiration was to corner his machine with the footboards raising sparks against the tarmac.

The ton-up boys grew up, the transport cafes on the old long-distance lorry routes closed, and the cafe racer died – almost. Until the late sixties, American road-racing was very much the poor cousin of its European counterpart for finesse, but very much the richer for its prizemoney. Europe's top riders regularly attended the major American events to 'show the Yanks the way home', generating a fresh interest in the sport which was to be compounded in 1971 by the setting-up of the Anglo-American Transatlantic Match Race Series.

Far left: this street racer is a Harley sportster with mild styling and an emphasis on speed rather than a far out appearance

Top left: last of the big Indians, an 80 cubic inch Big Chief sporting valenced fenders, a buddy seat, and four gallon petrol tanks

Above: a Triumph 650 engine from the 1950s in a light, rigid frame with just the bare essentials for rider comfort

Left: a turbocharged 750cc Honda tuned to drag race specification, whilst still remaining legal for the road where its performance is nothing short of devastating

Below: note the gold leaf on the tank of this chopped hog, an immaculate representation of a mid 1960s Dave Mann illustration

Searching for a new direction, several leading American custom builders recognised the scope offered by the distinct road racer styling and the cafe racer received a new lease of life. They had to dress it up a little of course, but, underneath the flamboyantly painted full fairing, behind the rose tinted windshield and between the rugged looking, cast magnesium alloy wheels, the cafe racer is alive and well.

Other members of the custom bike elite saw a great potential in the styling of the drag bike, a unique two-wheeled monster built for the prime purpose of propelling its rider from a standing start to the end of a measured quarter mile in the shortest possible time. Naturally enough, these machines were nothing more than incredible powerhouses, often turbo or supercharged, strung in the whispiest of frames between the front and rear wheel. West Coast designers Arlen Ness, Ron Nunes and Jim Jennings championed the radical 'street digger' look, while unbeknown to the others, and hundreds of miles from the custom bike mainstream, Portland, Oregon, exponent Barry Cooney also saw the digger as the solution to the chopper show bike impasse.

In the mid-seventies the street digger, or low rider as it is sometimes known, represents the most advanced stage of custom bike building. Ness and Cooney have joined forces to develop and refine their protégé; other builders, no less skilled or inventive in their art, have adapted the theme to suit their own particular themes, styles, dreams – and power units; for instance, the trike, a three-wheeled device fitted with a large V8 car engine. For, in a world now attuned to the rasp of multi-cylindered, Oriental muscle bikes, it is intriguing to find, nestling beneath the distinctive, angular lines of a Noss/Cooney fuel tank, a motor of long standing familiarity – a Harley-Davidson 74.   PM

Ruling with a Rod of Iron

It took the arrival of the Restrictive Trade Practices Act in the early 1960s to break the iron grip which the motor cycle manufacturers and suppliers 'trade union' had on the motor cycle trade and there are many still around who would argue that the trade is not necessarily better off for the transition.

Back at the start of the century, Britain was the hub of the motor cycle manufacturing world and it was not long before the manufacturers took the logical step of banding together to protect their mutual interests. In fact, the *original* trade association was the Cycle Manufacturers Association, for it was the bicycle that was the forerunner of the motor cycle and, indeed, formed the basis of most early motor cycles. They ran a national cycle show at Crystal Palace as early as 1893 and continued to do so up until 1903 but then the Cycle Manufacturers appeared to disappear, so to speak, and there was a gap of six years before the cycle and motor cycle trade got together to form the British Cycle and Motorcycle Manufacturers and Traders Union with the two-fold intention of running an annual motor cycle show and looking after the mutual interests of manufacturers and traders.

Students of vintage motor cycling will need no introduction to the name of the first President of the BCMMTU, Sir Charles Marston JP who manufactured the famous Marston Sunbeam in Wolverhampton. Over the years, the President has always been a well known figurehead and, although the names are perhaps less familiar to the modern rider, they all played a vital role in forging the British motor cycle industry into the once great body that it was.

Few will have heard of Seigfried Bettmann JP who was the President from 1928 to 1929, but this man came over from Germany to found the Triumph company and achieved the almost impossible by being elected Lord Mayor of Coventry during the World War I. He never lost his strong German accent and it says much for the character of the man that he became a legendary figure in the motor cycle trade and stories are still told of him. The following year his successor was a man whose family's initials are still to be seen on countless motor cycle tanks: it was George Stevens, MAIE, the name

being immortalised on the AJS. Norton never made the President's chair but a Norton man did finish up there, Gilbert Smith, who was in charge just before World War II, was elected from 1939 to 1940. Twenty-two years later, another well known name took the chair, Edward Turner of Triumph. In fact, the list of past Presidents reads like a 'Who's Who' in Vintage motor cycling.

It is different now of course. The 1977 President is the able and ebullient Peter Bolton of Puch, with Eric Sulley of Honda being vice-president. It could not have happened even twenty years ago for the simple reason that a British dominated association allowed foreign manufacturers, or, more accurately, the Concessionaires, no more than associate membership with no voting rights. There was, of course, a sound reason for this: ninety per cent of the motor cycle industry, perhaps a bit more, was home produced. It made sense to protect those interests and therefore the overseas competitor was, while not visibly discouraged, certainly not offered the welcome mat. Today, the boot is on the other foot with ninety per cent of the market being foreign-made, and a body representing only ten per cent of the market has little power. So, it was after a great deal of debate and heart searching that foreign manufacturers were allowed in with full voting rights. It was only after they had become established as a major threat, though, and some manufacturers *never* accepted that it was necessary.

They ruled with a rod of iron for the Association had the whole motor cycle industry sewn up with agreements, written and otherwise. In the old days any dealer who advertised even a pound off recommended list price would be marched up the steps of the industry's head office so fast (which is now situated at Starley House outside Coventry station) that his feet would not touch the ground. All prices had to be approved by the industry, agencies had to be approved and they were not scattered around like confetti, which explains why very often one reads of dealers finding it impossible to get agencies even as recently as fifteen years ago. It was not considered in the best interest of the motor cycle industry to have main agents on every street corner; no dealer could sell bikes unless he was in the union.

There was even an agreement to say that the industry were to be the only ones who could run a motor cycle show and, especially in pre-war days, these

Above: the first President of the
BCMMTU was Sir Charles Marston
JP. He was manufacturer of the Marston
Sunbeam in Wolverhampton

Top: Earls Court during the 1948 Motor
Cycle Show, when the British industry
flourished and many splendid makes were
still available

Above: pictured on a 750 Benelli are TV
personality Wei Wei Wong and 1975
Suzuki riders Barry Sheene and Tepi
Lansivuori at the 1975 Bike show

really *were* shows. Even the 1910 motor cycle show attracted no less than 283 machines. The show, held first at Olympia and later at Earls Court, was the major source of revenue to the Association and paid just all about their running costs. Individual members paid just £75 a year subscription, no matter how big, or small, they were; little wonder they kept the show on a tight string! In fact, the system is beginning to run that way again with the September Earls Court Show beginning to look as though it may regain its former glory but now it, too, is run by the industry. However, these days they use friendly persuasion to get exhibitors and do not close their doors to non members.

Yet another agreement was in operation to regulate works entries in major sporting events. The Association wanted to know who the works riders were and what manufacturer supported what event: no 'win' in an event could be advertised without the event being approved. Today's butterfly stars flitting from one highest bidder to the next would soon have found themselves out of business in the old days.

All that changed overnight with the arrival of the Restrictive Trade Practices Act, however. No longer was it possible to preset prices or to dictate to dealers their business so the British Cycle and Motorcycle Manufacturers and Traders Union (it was actually registered as a Trade Union in the early days) became the British Cycle and Motorcycle Industries Association, known almost immediately as the IA, and with it came a number of changing attitudes. The new law coincided with two other fundamental changes. The post-war boom in motor cycle sales had begun to slow down and the Japanese were beginning to make an impact on sales. The emphasis changed from ruling to educating and the IA realised that it was no longer riding the crest of a wave but fighting for survival. The first steps were an awareness that public relations were now important and for the first time ever a full time PRO was appointed, Hilary Watts. With the tactful and patient Hugh Palin as Director, the IA set about changing direction. The public and, more important, the government, had to be educated. The trade needed more and more information and this was available through the statistical section which, at this time, can tell those who wish to know just how many bikes of a particular make were sold in any given town the previous month. It began a trend that has seen today's organisation taking an increasingly responsible role in promoting the future of motor

cycling. They began an 'engines for schools' scheme with Norman Aubrey, who had succeeded Hilary Watts as Public Relations Officer, instigating a scheme that was to grow into a thriving organisation in its own right. This was STEP, Schools Traffic Education Programme, where the industry supplied motor cycles and knowledge to schools so that pupils could learn to ride motor cycles properly. STEP is now self governing but owes its birth to the motor cycle industry and its directors are all members of the industry.

Two years ago, the name of the Association changed once again. The paths of the bicycle and motor cycle, once so neatly entwined, were now diverging and it made sense to separate the operations. They became the Cycle Association and the Motorcycle Association (MCA) with the Cycle and Motor Cycle Association (the Industries Association part was dropped after a short time) remaining as the holding company for joint property, etc.

So, we arrive at the 1977 Motor Cycle Association, a democratic and responsible body that could be described as having three functions: 1) PR – publicising motor cycling in the broad sense; 2) providing information for industry on statistics, legislation, registrations, etc; 3) Political and Legislative – lobbying MPs, gaining political representation, etc.

In this sense, unlike the car bodies, it makes no sense to pressurise governments to apply import restrictions as most of their members are also importers. Finally, of course, there is still the running of motor cycle shows, an increasing part of the organisation. The income today is derived by a levy on machines sold. Also, £1 on every bike sold goes to the STEP scheme. The 1977 Director is Robert Liddell, with Ivor Davies running the Earls Court Show. They no longer have the power, or the desire, to march errant traders or manufacturers over the hallowed portals of Starley House, but they have a much more important function which is to promote the interest of motor cycling on every level. Perhaps there are those who hanker after the days of power and, just possibly, it could be argued that the motor cycle industry was stronger for it. It is a different world now, though, and manufacturers are not so easily dictated to. The present day Motorcycle Association certainly better serves the interests of the man who rides a motor cycle.   BP

Left and above left: the Earls Court Show attracts all the major manufacturers and their delectable models

This magnificent four-color encyclopedia is brought to you by Columbia House
in cooperation with Orbis Publishing Ltd., one of Great Britain's most enterprising publishers.
Rather than change any of the encyclopedia's authoritative international automotive text, we have
included a glossary of terms that will give you immediate American equivalents, and conversion tables
for the international metric system.

Glossary

BRITISH	AMERICAN	BRITISH	AMERICAN
Aerial	Antenna	Double knocker	Double overhead camshaft
Aero engine	Aircraft engine	Downdraught	Downdraft
Aerofoil	Airfoil	Dustbin	Garbage can
Aluminium	Aluminum	Dust excluder	Seal
Anti-froth baffle	Tank baffle	Dynamo	Generator
Anti-knock rating	Octane rating		
Apron	Skirt	Earth	Electrical ground
		Earthing strip	Ground wire
Back-to-front	Backwards	East-west mounting	Transverse mounting
Back to square one	Start over from the beginning	End-float	Runout
		Epicyclic gearbox	Planitary transmission
Badge engineering	Identical bikes with different nameplates (such as the BSA and Triumph brands)	Estate car	Station wagon
		Extreme-pressure lubricant	Heavy duty (gear) oil
Bang on	Exactly	Farrier	Blacksmith, horse shoer
Benzol	Benzene	First-motion shaft	Input shaft
Big-end	Larger (crankshaft) end of a connecting rod	Fit	Install
		Flat-out	Top speed
Bi-metal	Bi-metallic	Fore-and-aft mounting	Longitudinal mounting
Blow-back	Backfire in the intake manifold or carburetor	40 years on	40 years in the future
Blower	Supercharger	Gaiter	Rubber boot
Bottle-screw jack	Type of hydraulic jack	Gearbox	Transmission
Box spanner	Socket	Gearchange	Shift pedal or lever (n.) or shift (v.)
Brake horsepower (bhp)	Net horsepower (hp)		
Brake servo	Power brake	Glassfibre	Fiberglass
Bush	Bushing	Glass-reinforced plastic	Fiberglass
		Gudgeon pin	Piston or wrist pin
Capacity	Displacement		
Carburettor	Carburetor	Half-liners	Split shell bearings
Carcass	Tire body or plies	Half shaft	Axle shaft
Castellated nut	Castle nut	High tension	High voltage
Chain wheel	Sprocket	High-tension leads	Spark plug cables
Choke flap	Choke plate	Hose clip	Hose clamp
Clutch release bearing	Clutch throwout bearing		
Cogged belt	Rubber timing belt	Ignition harness	Ignition cable set
Collets	Split collar retainers	Immediately	As soon as
Conrod	Connecting rod	Indicators	Turn signals
Control box	Voltage regulator	Induction	Intake
Core plug	Freeze-out or Welsh plug	Inlet	Intake
Crash box	Non-synchromesh transmission	Jubilee clip	Brand of worm-drive hose clamp
Crocodile clip	Alligator clip	Judder	Shudder
Crown wheel	Ring gear	Jump leads	Jumper cables or wire
		Just on	Exactly
Damper	Shock absorber		
Decarbonise	Remove carbon deposits from combustion chamber	Kerb	Curb
		Knife cuts	Tire sipes
De-clutch	Disengage clutch	Layshaft	Countershaft
Decoke	See "Decarbonise"	Leads	Cables or wires
De-ionised water	Distilled water	Low-tension	Low voltage
Detonation	Pre-ignition	Main beam	High headlight beam, "brights"
Dipped headlight	Low beam		
Dipswitch	High/low beam switch	Marque	Brand, make
Directly	Right away	Midlands	English industrial center
DOE test	A state inspection	Mileage recorder	Odometer

Glossary

BRITISH	AMERICAN
Mileometer	Odometer
Mixture	Fuel-air mixture
Monobloc	Engine with crankcase and cylinder block cast in one piece
Monocoque	Frame constructed of sheetmetal box sections rather than tubes
Motor	Engine
Nave plate	Wheel cover, hubcap
Nil	Zero, nothing
Non-return valve	One-way valve
Number plate	License plate
One-lunger	Single-cylinder
One-off	One-of-a-kind
ONO	"Or near offer" (used in classified ads)
Opposite number	Equal, equivalent, mate
Overrun	Coasting in gear
Paraffin	Kerosene
Perspex	Plexiglas
Petroil	Gas and oil mixture
Petrol	Gasoline
Petrol pump	Fuel pump
Pillion	Passenger saddle or seat
Pinking	Pinging
Plunger	Detent ball
Pocketing	Excess valve seat wear
Pots	Cylinders
Production	Stock
Prop stand	Kick stand
Propeller shaft	Driveshaft
Purpose-built	Special
Quietening ramps	Low acceleration cam profile for quiet engine operation
RAC	Royal Automobile Club
Rear lamp	Tail light
Retrograde step	Step backwards
Rev counter	Tachometer
Ring spanner	Box wrench
Road roar	Tire noise
Rocker	Rocker arm
Rocker box	Rocker or valve cover
Rocker clearance	Valve clearance
Round	Around
Rubber solution	Rubber cement
Running-in	Break in
Running-on	Dieseling
Saloon	Sedan
Scheme	Plan, program
Screen	Windshield
Scuttle	Cowl

BRITISH	AMERICAN
Second-motion shaft	Countershaft
Sediment chamber	Trap
Self-locking nut	Locknut
Servo assisted	Power assisted
Shunt	Accident, bump, crash
Side-draught	Side draft
Side-valve engine	Flathead engine
Slow-running	Idle
Small-end	Smaller (piston) end of a connecting rod
Snap-in valve	Tubeless tire valve
Spade connector	Bayonet connector
Spanner	Wrench
Spigot	Pin
Spit-back	See "blow-back"
Split cones	Split collar retainers
Spot-on	Exactly
Squib	Auto seatback
5 star petrol	100 octane gasoline
4 star petrol	99-97 octane gasoline
3 star petrol	96-94 octane gasoline
2 star petrol	93-90 octane gasoline
Starting handle	Crank
Strangler flap	Choke plate
Sump	Oil pan
Swivel pin	Kingpin
Tab washer	Lock washer
Third-motion shaft	Output shaft
Throttle-stop screw	Idle speed screw
Throttle valve	Butterfly valve
Tick-over	Idle speed
Tin	Can
Tommy bar	Breaker bar, socket wrench
Top end	Cylinder head, or top speed
Trafficators	Early brand of turn signals
Twin-choke carburettor	Two-barrel carburetor
Tyre	Tire
Undo	Remove
Unsymmetrical	Asymmetrical
Venturi	Carburetor barrel
Volume-control screw	Idle mixture screw
Wheel brace	Lug wrench
Windscreen	Windshield
Wing	Fender
Wire wool	Steel wool
Works	Factory
Zinc-oxide grease	Bearing grease

Metric Equivalents
(Based on National Bureau of Standards)

Length

Centimeter (Cm.)	= 0.3937 in.	In.	= 2.5400 cm.
Meter (M.)	= 3.2808 ft.	Ft.	= 0.3048 m.
Meter	= 1.0936 yd.	Yd.	= 0.9144 m.
Kilometer (Km.)	= 0.6214 mile	Mile	= 1.6093 km.

Area

Sq. cm.	= 0.1550 sq. in.	Sq. in.	= 6.4516 sq. cm.
Sq. m.	= 10. 7639 sq. ft.	Sq. ft.	= 0.0929 sq. m.
Sq. m.	= 1.1960 sq. yd.	Sq. yd.	= 0.8361 sq. m.
Hectare	= 2.4710 acres	Acre	= 0.4047 hectare
Sq. km.	= 0.3861 sq. mile	Sq. mile	= 2.5900 sq. km.

Volume

Cu. cm.	= 0.0610 cu. in.	Cu. in.	= 16.3872 cu. cm.
Cu. m.	= 35.3145 cu. ft.	Cu. ft.	= 0.0283 cu. m.
Cu. m.	= 1.3079 cu. yd.	Cu. yd.	= 0.7646 cu. m.

Capacity

Liter	= 61.0250 cu. in	Cu. in.	= 0.0164 liter
Liter	= 0.0353 cu. ft.	Cu. ft.	= 28.3162 liters
Liter	= 0.2642 gal. (U.S.)	Gal.	= 3.7853 liters
Liter	= 0.0284 bu. (U.S.)	Bu.	= 35.2383 liters

$$\text{Liter} = \begin{cases} 1000.027 \text{ cu. cm.} \\ 1.0567 \text{ qt. (liquid) or } 0.9081 \text{ qt. (dry)} \\ 2.2046 \text{ lb. of pure water at 4 C} = 1 \text{ kg.} \end{cases}$$

Weight

Gram. (Gm.)	= 15.4324 grains	Grain	= 0.0648 gm.
Gram	= 0.0353 oz.	Oz.	= 28.3495 gm.
Kilogram (Kg.)	= 2.2046 lb.	Lb.	= 0.4536 kg.
Kg.	= 0.0011 ton (sht.)	Ton (sht.)	= 907.1848 kg.
Ton (met.)	= 1.1023 ton (sht.)	Ton (sht.)	= 0.9072 ton (met.)
Ton (met.)	= 0.9842 ton (lg.)	Ton (lg.)	= 1.0160 ton (met.)

Pressure

1 kg. per sq. cm.	= 14.223 lb. per sq. in.
1 lb. per sq. in.	= 0.0703 kg. per sq. cm.
1 kg. per sq. m.	= 0.2048 lb. per sq. ft.
1 lb. per sq. ft.	= 4.8824 kg. per sq. m.
1 kg. per sq. cm.	= 0.9678 normal atmosphere

$$1 \text{ normal atmosphere} = \begin{cases} 1.0332 \text{ kg. per sq. cm.} \\ 1.0133 \text{ bars} \\ 14.696 \text{ lb. per sq. in.} \end{cases}$$

How to Convert Metric Measurements to U.S. Equivalents

TO CONVERT:	TO:	MULTIPLY BY EXACTLY:	MULTIPLY BY APPROXIMATELY:
Millimeters (mm)	Inches (in.)	0.039	4/100
Centimeters (cm)	Inches (in.)	0.394	4/10
Meters (m)	Feet (ft.)	3.28	3¼
Meters (m)	Yards (yd.)	1.09	1-1/10
Kilometers (km)	Miles (mi.)	0.621	⅝
Kilometers per hour (kph)	Miles per hour (mph)	0.621	⅝
Kilometers per liter (kpl)	Miles per gallon (mpg)	2.352	2⅜
Square centimeters (cm²)	Square inches (sq. in.)	0.155	3/20
Square meters (m²)	Square feet (sq. ft.)	10.8	11
Square meters (m²)	Square yards (sq. yds.)	1.2	1¼
Cubic centimeters (cc)	Cubic inches (c. i.)	0.061	1/16
Liters (1000cc)	Cubic inches (c. i.)	61.025	61
Cubic meters (m³)	Cubic feet (cu. ft.)	35.3	35⅓
Cubic meters (m³)	Cubic yards (cu. yds.)	1.31	1⅓
Liters (l)	Pints (pt.)	2.11	2-1/10
Liters (l)	Quarts (qt.)	1.06	10/9
Liters (l)	U.S. gallons (gal.)	0.264	¼
Liters (l)	Imperial gallons	0.22	2/9
Imperial gallons	U.S. gallons	1.2	1¼
Miles per Imperial gallon	Miles per U.S. gallon	1.2	1¼
Grams (gm)	Ounces (oz.)	0.035	3/100
Kilograms (kg)	Pounds (lb.)	2.2	2¼
Metric tons	Tons	1.1	11/10
Hundredweight (cwt.)	Pounds (lb.)	112.0	—
Stone	Pounds (lb.)	14.0	—
Kilogram-meters (kg-m)	Foot-pounds (ft.-lb.)	7.232	7¼
Kilograms per square centimeter	Pounds per square inch (psi)	14.22	14¼
Metric horsepower (bhp DIN)	U.S. horsepower	0.9859	—

How to Convert U.S. Measurements to Metric Equivalents

TO CONVERT:	TO:	MULTIPLY BY EXACTLY:	MULTIPLY BY APPROXIMATELY:
Inches (in.)	Millimeters (mm)	25.4	25½
Inches (in.)	Centimeters (cm)	2.54	2½
Feet (ft.)	Meters (m)	0.305	3/10
Yards (yd.)	Meters (m)	0.914	9/10
Miles (mi.)	Kilometers (km)	1.609	8/5
Miles per hour (mph)	Kilometers per hour (kph)	1.609	8/5
Miles per gallon (mpg)	Kilometers per liter (kpl)	0.425	2/5
Square inches (sq. in.)	Square centimeters (cm²)	6.45	6½
Square feet (sq. ft.)	Square meters (m²)	0.093	1/10
Square yards (sq. yd.)	Square meters (m²)	0.836	4/5
Cubic inches (c. i.)	Cubic centimeters (cc)	16.4	16½
Cubic inches (c. i.)	Liters (1000cc)	0.164	4/25
Cubic feet (cu. ft.)	Cubic meters (m³)	0.0283	3/100
Cubic yards (cu. yd.)	Cubic meters (m³)	0.765	¾
Pints (pt.)	Liters (l)	0.473	½
Quarts (qt.)	Liters (l)	0.946	9/10
U.S. gallons (gal.)	Liters (l)	3.78	3¾
Imperial gallons (gal.)	Liters (l)	4.55	4½
Ounces (oz.)	Grams (gm)	28.4	28½
Pounds (lb.)	Grams (gm)	454.0	450
Pounds (lb.)	Kilograms (kg)	0.454	½
Foot-pounds (ft.-lb.)	Kilogram-meters (kg-m)	0.1383	3/20
Pounds per square inch (psi)	Kilograms per square cm	0.0703	7/100
U.S. horsepower	Metric horsepower (bhp DIN)	1.014	—